"[The Nayaswami Order] gave me the opportunity to make a commitment that I have yearned to make formally for a long time. . . . Already I feel my life changing and my consciousness expanding."
—Brahmacharini Pushpa

"I consider joining the new Renunciate Order to be one of the most important steps in my life. . . . The vow has brought more color, dimension, and texture to the tapestry of my spiritual efforts."
—Brahmacharini Liladevi

"These vows can be taken by a person of any religious faith, uniting our efforts to bless and uplift every being on this planet."
—Brahmachari Jagadeesh

"Swami Kriyananda has opened a door that I never thought would be available. . . . Since taking vows I have felt more acutely God's grace in my life. What great blessings have come!"
—Brahmacharini Surana

"Nayaswami Kriyananda has given all of us the spiritual tools and guidance in this new Renunciate Order to transcend our little egos. I have felt a deep connection to the spiritual power, magnetism, and bliss behind this initiation."
—Tyagini Chandi

"Since taking the Tyagi vow, I feel a sense of contentment and freedom. There is no need to worry anymore, but only to keep trying to be ever more centered in God."
—Tyagi Aumkara

"I feel such joy that keeps me connected to the Divinity within."
—Tyagini Gayatri

"After I took my . . . vows, . . I felt a real energy shift in my core. My heart feels open all of the time, and I accept judgment by others dispassionately as given to me by God for my spiritual growth and highest good. My only goal in life now is to please God alone."
—Tyagini Andrea

"Since taking the . . . vow, I feel more relaxed and self-accepting, yet with a more sincere dedication to finding God and serving the Guru's work as best as I can."
—Tyagi Dambara

"There is an ever-new, ever-increasing inner joy that I have been able to tap into at will since that very special day. . . . I'll never forget . . . the power and the softness during the ceremony. Just thinking about that magical, mystical moment brings tears to my eyes."

—Tyagi Gopal

"Religion often begins young, and ends up old and grey, but this Nayaswami Order has been colorfully created by the ever-free and fresh spirit of Swami Kriyananda."

—Tyagi Jayadev

"The renunciate vows given by Swami Kriyananda have greatly helped me re-focus on the Divine Goal. It's like finding a new, more detailed roadmap. I have felt very spiritually encouraged by the vow, which I embrace with all my heart."

—Tyagi Larry

"Over time I began to notice that I was more settled, joy was my frequent companion. I felt empowered to change, and became aware of a strength in the core of my being."

—Tyagini Lisa

"During the ceremony . . . tears filled my eyes. I felt reverence and gratitude as well as the strength and conviction that living my life for God is truly the only reason I'm here on this planet."

—Tyagini Jivani

"My experience during the ceremony was one of extraordinary lightness. I felt a blessing coming from another plane of existence and an assurance that this was right for me. I knew that God was there to help me, and that it would be no burden."

—Nayaswami Mukti

"Since formally taking the Nayaswami vow . . . I can sincerely say that I feel changed forever, uplifted, and strengthened in my determination to live for God alone."

—Nayaswami Savitri

"The words of the vows of the Order are imbued with spiritual power. I have found that my vow as a Nayaswami is helping me untangle my Self from the post of ego. I find that I am ever more focused on God in my heart."

—Nayaswami Padma

"My heart is filled with joy at the vast potential for freedom in this sacred order."

—Nayaswami Nalini

"Taking the Nayaswami vow has shone a spotlight in my consciousness upon who I really am, what my only purpose in life is: to seek God and to serve as His channel of blessing to all."
—Nayaswami Nishkama

"This vow has a power that inspires greater devotion than I have known before. As it has strengthened my will, it has lifted my spirit as well."
—Nayaswami Surendra

"The evening I took my vows, I felt such joy in my heart, the deepest joy I have ever experienced. I feel God's presence guiding and uplifting me, and I know [it all] comes from God's hand."
—Nayaswami Tushti

"The new Renunciate Order has given energy and focus to my spiritual life and deepened my commitment to God and Guru."
—Nayaswami Nakin

"The vows . . . brought more strength and power into my life, along with a feeling that God and Guru were closer than ever. Since the vows, I feel that same strength within me, lifting me up, encouraging me to meet all challenges that come in life."
—Nayaswami Lalita

"The bliss that radiated from Swamiji as he initiated each person, and the deep love in his eyes for each soul who came before him, were indescribable. One felt the perfection of God's love, and the radiance and deep spiritual vibrations that are emanating from it now are touching everyone."
—Nayaswami Durga

"While [the vows] are uniquely personal on a day-to-day, moment-by-moment level, their power is greatly magnified by the fact that they speak to souls of any path who want to live for God Alone."
—Nayaswami Maria

"In my mind I was not sure that I was qualified to take the Vow of Complete Renunciation, but my heart told me it was the right thing to do. . . . Soon [after taking the vow] I was awed by waves of powerful blessings flowing in all aspects of my life."
—Nayaswami Sudarshan

"What the Nayaswami Renunciate vows mean to me is the freedom to seek the deepest relationship with God of which I am capable."
—Nayaswami Janakidevi

"There is an amazing grace that comes with the taking of this vow."
—Nayaswami Santoshi

"Every morning when I review the vow and dedicate myself anew to trying to bring these beautiful ideals more and more into my daily life, I feel a growing happiness and freedom."
—Nayaswami Maitri

"I feel a much deeper devotion, and feel God's presence in my life more deeply. I love the freedom I have felt in releasing so many . . . attachments . . . to things and the results of my actions."
—Nayaswami Gloria

"I woke up out of a deep sleep, sat up in bed and announced . . . 'I'm going to take . . . the Nayaswami vow!' The whole focus of my life switched instantaneously and dramatically. My consciousness shifted. Everything around me seemed brighter and clearer."
—Nayaswami Ruth

"Swamiji's inspiration to start this new Order in [St. Francis's Assisi] was so perfect. This is not a sectarian order, but a guideline that all devotees can use for understanding and deepening their own journey along the spiritual path."
—Nayaswami Vijay

"I believe this ceremony has [the] power to transform lives."
—Nayaswami Nivritti

"There is tremendous spiritual power in the Nayaswami Order, and people have experienced deep blessings that have completely transformed their consciousness after inwardly embracing the vows of the Order. . . . Virtually every sincere seeker who has joined the Order has reported . . . transformative changes in his life."
—Nayaswami Bharat

For more information on the New Renunciate Order,
please visit www.nayaswami.org.

A Renunciate Order
for the New Age

A Renunciate Order
for the New Age

Swami Kriyananda

Crystal Clarity Publishers
Nevada City, California

Crystal Clarity Publishers, Nevada City, CA 95959
Copyright © 2010 by Hansa Trust
All rights reserved. Published 2010

Printed in USA
ISBN13: 978-156589-252-1

Cover photograph by Andrea Roach
Cover design by Renée Glenn Designs
Interior layout and design by Crystal Clarity Publishers

Library of Congress Cataloging-in-Publication Data

Kriyananda, Swami.
A Renunciate Order for the New Age / Swami Kriyananda.
p. cm.
ISBN 978-1-56589-252-1 (tradepaper)
1. Spiritual life. 2. Monastic and religious life. I. Title.

BP605.S4K76 2010
294.5'657—dc22

2009049174

www.crystalclarity.com
800-424-1055
clarity@crystalclarity.com

Contents

Preface

Renunciation has ceased to command the respect it once had. Spirituality is on the rise, but many convents and monasteries stand empty. What people want now is a path where Spirit and Nature work in harmony, not in opposition to one another.

Timeless principles, however, are not created by popular vote. Truth simply Is.

Renunciation remains the heart and soul of the spiritual life. The problem is not with the principle itself, but the way it has been misunderstood and wrongly practiced. Renunciation has become defined by what you give up, or, even worse, by what God takes away.

True renunciation is not a loss, it is an expansion to Infinity. Joy and renunciation are two sides of the same coin. To suppress the ego is not the same as transcending it.

The origin of this book is auspicious. A miracle healing was needed before it could be written.

There has always been something mysterious about Swami Kriyananda's health. His body seems to be a battleground where the forces of Light and Dark meet. The battle is not about him personally, but for the work his guru, Paramhansa Yogananda, has commissioned him to do. The only way to describe it is "Satan tries to stop him." Often his most creative periods are paired with enormous physical challenges.

Swamiji cheerfully dismisses the trials of his body as merely the *tapasya* needed to establish his guru's work in this world. (*Swamiji* means *respected teacher*; *tapasya* is a Sanskrit word meaning both *austerity* and *devotion.*)

Still, the effort has taken its toll. No physical body lasts forever. It is of no consequence to Swamiji whether he lives or dies; long ago he surrendered his life to his guru.

Especially since he moved to India in 2003, Swamiji has had one health crisis after another. Often he has told his Indian audiences, "I'm not going to live much longer," hoping to inspire them to act quickly to build the work while he was still there to help them. Certain "readings," including the ancient *Book of Bhrigu*, implied that his eighty-third birthday, May 19, 2009, might be his last.

Two days after that birthday, he was scheduled to fly from India to Europe. That morning he had some symptoms of a stroke: difficulty breathing, speaking, and so weak he had to be fed like a baby.

Ordinarily, no one would travel in such a condition. But persevering against obstacles has always strengthened Swamiji rather than weakened him. Once a project or transition is completed, usually health returns.

But this time it didn't happen. Even weeks later, at home now in Ananda Assisi, the crisis continued. Rarely had he been so weak for so long. Someone had to be with him twenty-four hours a day.

It was June 6; I was on the afternoon shift. A few friends were coming over in the late afternoon, so when Swamiji went to take a nap, he asked me to wake him in time for their coming.

At 3:00 he was still sound asleep. Reluctantly I woke him and helped him sit up on the side of the bed. Traditionally, swamis wear orange, but I chose for him a blue shirt instead, thinking the color would lift his spirits. As I was doing up the buttons I said casually, "This blue is so exquisite. You should change the swami color from orange to blue."

With great seriousness, he replied, "I am thinking of doing that."

I helped him into the living room, then went back to get something from the closet. When I returned a moment later, he was stretched out on the couch, hands folded across his heart, looking up at the ceiling. I thought he might be dead. In fact, that may be when the miracle happened.

To my great relief, he began to speak, introducing the ideas that are now this book: *A Renunciate Order for the New Age*. After a few moments, he paused, then quietly, with great force, declared, "*This* is what Satan was trying to stop."

From that moment he began to get well.

In the evening he called a group together to talk about the new order. Already he had written most of the first chapter of this book. Just hours before he couldn't button his own shirt. Now he was launching a revolution in renunciation for the New Age.

"I entered a state of intense bliss," Swamiji said later, about this sudden change. "I told Divine Mother, 'I'm ready to go and I am happy to stay, if You have more work for me to do here.' It didn't matter at all to me. When I came out of that state, I began to get well." When he left Italy a few weeks later, he didn't even bring his cane.

"I feel ageless," Swamiji says. "I don't identify with myself in any way now. It seems God has extended my life in order to do this work. It was a miracle healing."

In the forty years that I have known Swamiji, his

prodigious creativity has been nothing less than awe-inspiring. Books, music, communities, schools, retreats—a spiritual network that spans the globe. Often in my enthusiasm for some particular expression I have been tempted to declare: "This is it! This is his spiritual legacy."

Of course, to say that is like defining the ocean by what you can see from the beach.

Still, folly though it may be, I dare to say that, in its cumulative effect, *A Renunciate Order for the New Age* may be one of Swamiji's most important contributions to the bringing in of a New Age. For it gives to truth seekers everywhere the courage, the clarity, and the way to open their hearts to God.

Nayaswami Asha

Chapter One

My Intention

My intention in these pages is to propose a new model of renunciation for this age of energy. Swami Sri Yukteswar Giri, my *paramguru* (guru's guru), described it as such, giving it its ancient Sanskrit name, *Dwapara*. Having explained this matter already in several of my other writings (notably in *Religion in the New Age*), I'd rather proceed here at once to my main subject: renunciation in this age of energy.

The monastic order of swamis in India was founded, or rather reorganized, many centuries ago by the first, or *adi*, Swami Shankara. The age in which he lived was known as *Kali*, or dark (literally, "black") *Yuga* (age). It was far more materialistic than the age in which we live today. Shankara wrote rules and ideals for his renunciate order that were appropriate for those times, when society faced a different set of realities.

People weren't nearly so mobile then as they are today. Travel, by present-day standards, was very slow. There were no motorized vehicles, no airplanes, no steamships. People's mental horizons, too, were narrowly circumscribed. To accomplish anything, one's self-definition, too, had to be narrow.

To find God, or to realize the Divine Presence in one's life, was almost impossible for those whose lives were not specifically devoted to spiritual progress. Those who lived in the world, who engaged in profit, and particularly who were married and had families, simply could not expand their horizons to include the divine search.

In the Christian world, renunciates sometimes went so far as to have themselves walled up in cells, with only little openings through which food was passed. To find God, renunciation of all distractions had, in fact, to be complete, for every attachment to the world needed to be shattered. In India, renunciates were told not to find enjoyment in anything, even in a beautiful sunset. They were expected to go by foot from place to place; never to stay in one place more than three days; and be careful not to regard anyone or any place as their own. "*Neti, neti*"—literally, "Not this; not that"— was the common practice for the spiritual seeker. It was a way of rejecting everything in the manifested universe as false.

In both East and West it was common—indeed, the practice was honored—for monks to beg their food from house to house; to accept only enough food for one meal; and to carry no money in their purse.

Jesus Christ was a renunciate in this sense. So also was St. Francis of Assisi. And so also have been many Christian saints, who have dedicated themselves to "the imitation of Christ." St. Francis used to say that he was wedded to "Lady Poverty." Paramhansa Yogananda, who spoke of St. Francis as his "patron saint," said, "I prefer the term, 'Lady Simplicity.'" Sri Yogananda's view of renunciation was much more moderate than what was practiced in Kali Yuga. The old way had been right for those days, when mankind's awareness was much narrower. Kali Yuga was a time of rigid dogmas amounting to dogmatism, rigid social codes, and a rigid concept of matter itself, which was considered fixed, solid, and essentially immutable.

In modern times, matter has been found to consist of subtle energy vibrations. People's thinking is more fluid, more intuitive, more centered in principle than in outer forms.

The swami order (unlike Catholic monasticism) did not include women. Indeed, it would not have been appropriate for women in those days to roam the roads freely, as swamis were supposed to do.

Nowadays, although lip service is still given to the ancient practices, most swamis do in fact own a little money and even property. They are not criticized for doing so, provided they use their possessions for the benefit of others. Swamis no longer live in stark poverty. In keeping with our times, their renunciation is, outwardly speaking, more moderate. Inwardly, it is more focused on right attitudes. In this age, mental discipline is understood to be more important than outer, physical austerities.

At the same time, the need of the hour is to deepen this attitude. Freedom from anger, hate, pride, and desire is more important than renunciation of outer, material involvements.

Most of the ancient restrictions are viewed today in the light rather of sacred tradition than of actual reality. Many swamis, if they own property, emphasize the importance of inward non-attachment to it. Few renunciates today wander the highways, where they'd anyway face the risk of being run over by a motor vehicle, or asphyxiated by motor fumes. Most modern-day renunciates dwell in ashrams like their Western counterparts, who live in monasteries. When they travel, they usually go by car, train, ship, or airplane. Were they to beg their food from door to door, they'd very probably be treated as mere panhandlers.

It must be understood that the main purpose of those ancient rules was to help the renunciate to develop non-attachment. Today, people also realize that desires, when utterly denied, may easily become stronger and take deeper root in the heart than if they are moderately satisfied. In fact, the Bhagavad Gita counsels moderation in all things. And whereas non-attachment to things is easier if the things themselves are entirely out of reach anyway—such as, let us say, a ride in a UFO—the desire for things that *are* available may actually be fanned by total denial.

To put it more concretely, I have noted that, despite the widespread notion (in India especially) that poor people are more likely to become saints than those who are well to do, in fact, those who go to the saints, and indeed the saints themselves, seem almost always to come from middle-class or upper-middle-class homes. The poor are forced by circumstances to devote all their time and energy to basic survival, leaving almost no time or strength to address their spiritual needs.

It must be understood, further, that non-attachment itself is not the goal of renunciation, the supreme purpose of which is to give one the freedom to devote himself primarily to his spiritual search. The real delusion to be overcome is the bondage of ego-identity. The true goal of renunciation is to help one to rid himself of that self-limiting identity.

The word "swami" means, literally, "he who is one with himself." The title is usually, of course, only an affirmation of that ideal. Few swamis have actually attained the goal. Still, by firm dedication to God alone they should be well on the way to divine attainment before they take their swami vows.

In this regard especially, I am bound to say that I have met many swamis in India who seemed to me even, perhaps, unnaturally arrogant, as well as being by no means free from anger and personal ambition. The fact that they have outwardly renounced worldly associations seems to have placed them, in their own eyes, on a higher plateau than mere *samsaris*, or worldly people. I have often wondered: What use, to them, a renunciation that inflates the very ego it is supposed to annihilate? Again, what use, to them, their orange robes—if they can still get angry?

The renunciate should indeed eschew worldly involvements, but he should not despise the countless ignorant, struggling egos who are still involved in *samsara*. *Maya* (delusion) is very subtle. Often it ensnares people through their very rationale for escaping it.

There is a story in Indian tradition of a hermit who was disturbed during meditation one day by the cawing of a crow. He glanced up at it in anger, and it fell immediately to the ground, dead. "What power I've acquired!" thought the hermit proudly. A *devata* (angel) just then appeared to him and said, "You think yourself so highly advanced, but there is one who is more advanced than you, living in the town near here. You could learn much from her."

"A woman! Is that possible?"

"Go and see," said the angel, and instructed him where to find her. The hermit entered the town and, after some time, arrived at a very ordinary home; he considered it beneath him even to enter there. He therefore called out, and a woman answered from within, "I will come to you shortly. I am busy just now, serving my husband."

"She's married!" thought the hermit indignantly. "How could a married person possibly be on a higher spiritual plane than I?" Just then she called out, "Be patient, Sir. I am not your crow!"

So she knew about that episode! He decided to wait. When at last she emerged, she spoke from a level of wisdom that did indeed prove enlightening for him.

Humbled, he returned to his place of seclusion. The angel hadn't yet finished with him, however. Appearing to him a second time, he said, "You've learned something, but not yet everything that you need to know. There is another person in town from whom you still have much to learn." The angel instructed him where to go.

The hermit returned to town. This time, he found himself entering the lowest section, where the butchers and leather workers worked and lived.

"How could any saint possibly live here?" he marveled. When he reached the house of the person he was to see, he found it belonged to a young man who, again, hadn't time for him at the moment; he was busy serving his parents.

When finally the youth appeared, the hermit learned from him that to do one's God-allotted duty is the highest calling, and should never be despised. The important thing is not to become *attached* to one's duty.

This was, for him, a vitally important lesson. Many renunciates, in forsaking worldly involvement, overlook their duty to serve their broader family of mankind. The renunciate should offer back gratefully to this world the energy and blessings he receives from God. His renunciation should be a means of *expanding* his sense of selfhood.

To achieve this end, he must develop an attitude of selfless service, rendered to others according to his own ability. If he can sit all day in *effective* meditation, that may in fact be the highest service he can offer. His meditation, however, should be practiced with an attitude of self-offering to God, and a desire for the upliftment of all mankind, not with a desire only for personal (even though spiritual) gain.

The supreme task all men are given who would become worthy of the kingdom of God is to expand their ego-consciousness from its pristine finitude to the vast Self of which the ego is but a little part—a mere grain of sand on a vast beach surrounding the ocean of cosmic consciousness. Man must seek infinite self-expansion.

In India, tradition has inculcated in people the idea that service to those who are more highly spiritual than oneself is a way of evolving personally. It is a good tradition. Merely to have embraced formal renunciation, however, in no way guarantees high attainment. Many swamis and other renunciates, on finding people eager to serve them, develop an *expectation* of being served, and in time come to assume that such service is their natural due. In this attitude they strengthen, but don't expand, their ego-identity.

Thus, in creating a new renunciate order, I want to address above all the fundamental purpose behind the monastic life itself: transcendence, and the attainment of oneness with the greater Self of all: God. As Paramhansa Yogananda wrote in his great poem, "*Samadhi*": "Myself, in everything, enters the Great Myself."

When my Guru, in 1950, placed me in charge of the other monks in his order, our renunciate way of life had not yet been developed. He himself had given us only two rules: no speaking at the table during mealtimes, and no intermingling of the sexes. The time had come, I saw, to give the order more specific form. To me fell the job of organizing our way of life.

As I did so, my Guru told me, "Don't make too many rules: It destroys the spirit."

7

Monasticism in the West has been based, by contrast, almost entirely on "the Rule." In my new position, I tried to avoid this negative emphasis. Traditionally, the monastic is told, "Don't do this; don't do that; don't go here; don't go there; sit properly; direct your gaze humbly to the ground." All these, and similarly restrictive injunctions cause the monastic to lose that cheerful confidence in God which alone enables one's spirit to soar.

When I met my Guru, he gave me his unconditional love, and asked me to give him mine in return. I did so with all my heart. Next, he asked me to give him my unconditional obedience. Desperate though I was to be accepted by him, I had to be truthful. Therefore I asked him, "What if, occasionally, I think you are wrong?" He replied, "I will never ask anything of you that God Himself does not tell me to ask." With that understanding, I gave him my unconditional obedience also.

Obedience is traditionally demanded of monks, especially in the West. However, though my Guru had placed me in charge of the monks, I did not feel competent to make such a request of them. After all, wasn't I myself still struggling to come out of the pit of delusion? I feared the development of attitudes in myself of superiority and condescension. Rather, therefore, I chose to be in a position where I could learn from anyone with something worthwhile to teach me. Therefore I told my fellow monks, "I won't ask your obedience. All I ask is your intelligent *cooperation*. And I promise in return to cooperate with you in anything you ask of me, provided it doesn't go against either my principles or our monastic calling."

Ten years after our Guru's passing, I was dismissed from the order. My superiors had wanted me to accept blindly, in a passive spirit of submissiveness, their every wish for me. My difficulty was that our Guru had instructed me personally as to what my mission would be. Those instructions conflicted in many ways with what they asked of me. After some years of doing my best to obey them, while at the same time trying to fulfill what he himself had asked of me, I finally had no choice but to accept that he, not they, was my Guru. I remembered him, moreover, having once written, "Strict obedience to a person of God-realization leads to inner freedom, but unquestioning obedience to someone who is not enlightened may lead to further bondage."

My road through life, based not only on my Guru's stated wishes for me, but also on what he perceived to be my own nature, has been to apply his teachings creatively, as I've understood them, to the needs of others. Without such creative application, no one can progress very far on the path.

The form of renunciation I propose here, then, encourages creativity *of the right sort.*

As the reader may know, I have composed a fair amount of music in my life. Years ago, an Ananda member decided to write music of his own. (In fact, his "compositions" were derivative in style, and by no means inspired.) He said to me, "*You* know what it's like to express yourself creatively; it's something you just *have* to do." I replied, "No, I know no such thing. I've never written even a note of music to express myself. To me, music composition has been a service to others. I've never done anything out of personal compulsion. If I'd never composed a melody, or written a single book, in my life, I'd feel just as inwardly fulfilled as I do now."

In fact, when I was young I aspired to be a playwright. My purpose was to share the truth with others.

When I realized that I myself didn't know the truth, I decided, "Why flood the world with my ignorance?" I gave up writing altogether. Years later, as a disciple of my Guru, I felt I had reached the point where I was now ready—with a measure of fear and trembling—to begin to carry out his instructions to me to write. Since then, though I've had no access to the world of the theater, I have been able to write two or three pieces for the stage.

My goal in everything I've done has been to achieve inner freedom, and to inspire others in the same direction. Never have I tried to "express myself." This little self of mine, this ego, is something I've tried my best to escape—not in a spirit of self-negation, but of reaching out to embrace the divine universe, in God, as my own.

The form of renunciation I propose in these pages encourages creativity primarily with a view to developing in people their own, innate sense of right and wrong, and not as an encouragement to egoic self-expression. What I encourage also is the submission of their will to what is right in everything, without relying excessively on the opinions of others—that is to say, to listen respectfully to their opinions, but to accept only those which their own intuition endorses.

My superior, during the years when I lived at Mt. Washington, tried once to get me to work in the print-shop. (I wonder if she didn't try this ploy partly to get me out of her hair, with all my suggestions for how to expand the work!) Her plan was diametrically opposed, however, to what Master himself had told me to do.* She wanted to suppress me, whereas he kept

* He'd said to me, "Your work in this life is lecturing, writing, and editing." He didn't add, "forming communities," but had he done so, my own determination to work in that direction would have formed prematurely. As it was, I began creating communities as a natural consequence of the

encouraging me in my creativity. Had I not received his personal counsel, I might have allowed my creativity to be stifled, to the lasting detriment of my spiritual progress. Indeed, in looking back I realize now that my superior would never have allowed me the time even to write serious books. And the editor-in-chief would never have published any book I did write.* The editor once said to me regarding her neglect toward editing Master's own books, "What more do people need? They have all the books they need for their spiritual advancement anyway." When she threw me out, she tried to discourage me altogether from writing anything, and insisted, "Everything you could possibly write has been done before!"

In Western monasteries, it is usual to suppress creativity. I have read of novice nuns being told to plant flowers in the ground *upside down*, solely to educate them in mindless obedience. Adherence to such instructions, offensive as it is to all reason, not only suppresses the ego, but suffocates one's spiritual aspiration. Blind obedience deprives one of common sense, which, St. Teresa of Avila said, is even more important than devotion. (Devotion, she said, can be developed, but common sense is something one either has or doesn't have.) A monastery that tries to reduce everyone to a single expression of spirituality is an offense against Nature itself, which never repeats anything exactly, not even a snowflake!

There is much in traditional monasticism, both East and West, that actually serves to impede true spiritual

---

other work I was doing. In answer to his statement that my work would be writing, I asked him, "Sir, haven't you, yourself, already written everything that needs to be written?" In answer, he looked a little shocked and said, "Don't say that! *Much* more is needed!"

* Though she did publish a little book I wrote about our Guru's childhood: *Stories of Mukunda.*

progress. In India, the worst aspect of monasticism is, in my view, that it encourages pride. In the West, the worst aspect of monasticism is that it tries to get people to overcome the ego by suppressing it, instead of encouraging self-transcendence. As India's best-loved scripture, the Bhagavad Gita, puts it, "How is suppression (even) possible?" (3:33)

It is true that one who would find God must renounce everything—including, above all, his sense of having a separate individuality. Such renunciation, however, can be accomplished only by one's own free will. Moreover, what renunciation of the ego makes possible is the free expression of God's unique manifestation, as one's own self.

In the *Mahabharata*, the ego is represented by "Grandfather" Bhishma, who received the boon of not dying until he relinquished his own body. Indeed, the ego is the last delusion to disappear. It can only be transcended by self-offering into the Infinite. With the final surrender of the last shreds of ego-consciousness comes an oceanic bliss, spreading out to embrace the universe. The classical Christian belief in negative submissiveness to God suggests someone on his knees, bowed to the ground and casting dust repeatedly onto his own head. I suggest that one accomplishes nothing by this attitude—except, perhaps, a focus on dust (sin, in other words) and on one's own head! True humility is complete self-forgetfulness. Indeed, it reminds me of something my Guru once said, "How can there be humility, when there is no consciousness of self?"

The Buddhist concept of *nirvana*, which has been thought to mean "nothingness," is another attempt at explaining the ego's essential non-reality. What most Buddhists don't understand is that in "no-thingness" the soul finds absolute bliss. One wonders, in fact, whether *anyone* would willingly seek complete self-annihilation, unless he believed also in a higher Self into which his soul would be absorbed. The negative goal, as it is commonly understood, sounds suspiciously like the "cop-out" of suicide.

The *nirvana* Buddha experienced, as Paramhansa Yogananda explained, is that state of inner freedom in which no attachment or desire remains rippling over the surface of the sea of one's consciousness. The ego has vanished altogether. Into this initial emptiness there rushes, filling the void, the oceanic bliss of *Satchidananda*: ever-existing, ever-conscious, ever-new Bliss, which was Swami Shankara's definition of God.

Many years ago, in Thailand, I read an official Buddhist tract which compared what it considered the Buddhist ideal of *nirvana* with the Hindu belief in absolute bliss (*Satchidananda*). The essay stated (I paraphrase): "While it is true that *nirvana* is preceded by a fleeting moment of bliss, this experience is followed by another, of complete nothingness." This teaching was, of course, quite the opposite of Paramhansa Yogananda's experience, and of every other great master's, anywhere! What the tract described, however, was *modern* Buddhism. It was not the teaching of Gautama, the Buddha. This was the counterpart of Western "Churchianity."

Contemplating this supposed difference, however, one wonders: Whence did the Buddha derive his universally admired compassion? One can imagine compassion being rooted in absolute bliss. One cannot imagine its being rooted in total unawareness! How, indeed, would anyone, *ever*, sincerely devote his life to attaining nothingness? Small wonder that modern

Buddhists uphold so fervently the ideal of Bodhisattva*
(which, to yogis, is the state of *jivan mukta*)!

Modern Christianity, too, circumscribes drastically
the teachings of Jesus Christ. *Churchianity*, as my
Guru called it, describes the highest heaven as being
a place where the free soul continues to live through
eternity in a separate body, forever locked in its own individual ego. A certain theologian once wrote words to
the effect that, "To the Christian, an impersonal state
in which all forms ceased to exist would be abhorrent."
What that man should have said, of course, was, "To
the *ego*, such a state is abhorrent." Indeed, to the ego,
anything that threatens its existence is abhorrent.

Swami Sri Yukteswar compared the ego to a caged
bird: After years of confinement, the bird may imagine
it *belongs* in that cage; it can't imagine itself soaring
high up in the sky.

The true saints in Christianity, however, have realized Bliss as the only reality in existence. They have
said so in many ways, in person and in their writings.†
Love might be described as the first manifestation of
bliss. St. Jean Vianney, a great saint in France, once
stated, "If you knew how much God loves you, you
would *die* for joy!"

The goal of renunciation is to help one to achieve
complete absorption in that Bliss. Therefore swamis
in India have commonly assumed names that end in
the word, "*ananda*" (bliss). In India, the main criterion
of renunciation has been non-attachment to money,
place, and possessions. Had Swami Shankara taught
the need to dissolve the ego, how many people would

---

* One who defers entering into *nirvana* in order to continue serving
humanity.

† I have listed a number of their statements in this regard in my book,
The New Path.

14

have even understood him? Only in the present age, with science's discovery that matter itself has no permanent reality,* is it possible to understand intellectually, at least, that the individual ego, too, may not really exist. Swami Shankara *did* describe all creation as being only a dream of God's, but still it was not possible in his time for even profound thinkers to see the human ego itself as being real only as a dream of God's.

Generally speaking, in India—judging by my own observation—the goal of spiritual striving does not seem to have been transcendence of the ego. Many renunciates, no doubt sincere in their disclaimers of attachment to money, place, possession, and position, still place great emphasis on their own authority, especially in spiritual matters.

I see no reason to think that modern swamis have compromised their ideals by owning possessions, or by having fixed places to live. The times have simply changed. The spiritual need of our age, and a goal to which everyone can now aspire, is the further understanding that outward forms and distinctions have no reality at all except as manifestations of something formless and insubstantial.

As for Western monasticism, imagine anyone these days going from house to house with a begging bowl! There simply has to be a suitable cultural setting for such practices. And to try to *create* such a setting would require more energy, and produce fewer gains, than would be worthwhile.

My fellow disciples in our Guru's organization have interpreted his mission as being above all to establish a monastery, one conducted along the old lines. I see

* For although matter cannot be destroyed, it *can* be dissolved back into its essential reality, which is energy.

15

his actual mission, instead, as having been to address the needs of an entire society—indeed, a whole civilization. He was sent to effect fundamental changes at every level of human life.

For spiritual seekers, monasteries of the traditional sort—especially because of their emphasis on strict obedience to rule and central authority—have become passé. In Italy, which was at one time the seat of Christian monasticism, huge monasteries today contain only a handful of monks, most of them—dare I say it, at my own age of eighty-three?—doddering old men in their eighties. Paramhansa Yogananda introduced countless innovations in this age. His own organization, however, has clung to Kali Yuga forms and traditions. It claims that he came for no grand, world-changing purpose—though he himself often, with great fervor, stated, "You have no idea what a *great* work this is! It is destined to change the whole world!" Fortunately for the future of his mission, my senior fellow-disciples dismissed me as a traitor! They were right: I was not loyal to their antiquated interpretation of the scope of his vision. Since then I have been able to pursue the path he himself indicated to me personally: a path leading straight into *Dwapara Yuga*, and to incalculably greater freedom at all levels.

My fellow disciples have gone back with a vengeance to the concept of complete monastic obedience. No one is allowed to question any directive from above, lest he be labeled disloyal and a troublemaker. Virtually every decision gets made by the board of directors.

Years ago, a door between the guest kitchen and the dining room at the SRF retreat in Encinitas got broken. Six months later, when my informant left there and came to live at Ananda, the door had yet to be repaired because permission to fix it had not yet come down from the board of directors in Los Angeles. How can any spiritual work flourish in such a suffocating atmosphere?

Swami Sri Yukteswar listed "pride of pedigree" among what he described as "meannesses of the heart." This aspect of pride has been anathema to organized religion everywhere. The thought that one person is better than others simply because he holds a higher position than they in the organization, or because he has been years longer on the path, is simply one of the pitfalls into which the ego can all too easily fall. Renunciates would do well to remind themselves constantly that he is most worthy in God's eyes who considers himself least among men.

In truth, most of the Master's highly advanced disciples were either married or had at one time been married. To treat the married state as something "beyond the pale" for the sincere seeker is a sign of pride, not of wisdom.

What I propose to do here is open the path of renunciation to all those, whether married or single, who deeply yearn to know God.

What, then, are the marks of those whom I'd consider worthy of being accepted as true renunciates? They would be those who have achieved noteworthy progress toward the attainment of the following virtues:

1. They have no, or very few, attachments or desires.

2. They are without anger. (Anger appears in the heart when one's desires are thwarted.)

3. They accept without prejudice whatever life gives them, and live by the principle, "What comes of itself, let it come."

4. They never seek to justify or defend themselves, but accept all judgment by others dispassionately,

17

as experiences given them by God for their higher good.

5. They keep in their hearts primarily the company of God.

6. They are indifferent to others' opinions of them.

7. They work without personal motive, to please God alone.

8. They are impersonal in the sense of wanting nothing for themselves, but never in the sense of being indifferent to the needs of others.

9. They see all beings as striving toward the attainment of *Satchidananda*: ever-existing, ever-conscious, ever-new Bliss, no matter how presently misguided the efforts of some people may be. Thus, they feel kinship with everyone, and with all life.

10. They accept nothing as their own, but only as being "on loan" to them, for the benefit of others.

11. They view pleasure and pain equally, as opposite (or dual) expressions of eternal, divine bliss.

12. They have meditated daily for years.

13. Because they are always happy in themselves, they are impervious to insults, outer suffering, failure, defeat, or disaster. They strive to live the ideal that Paramhansa Yogananda voiced when he said, "You should be able to stand unshaken amidst the crash of breaking worlds!"

14. They strive to love God unceasingly, and ever more deeply, in a spirit of utter openness to be guided by His will.

Chapter Two

The Dilemma

For years, a certain friend of mine asked me repeatedly to make him a swami. At last I said to him, "I couldn't rightly give you that advantage over the leaders at Ananda." He dropped the subject, but I myself was unable to do so.

Indeed, this has been, for many years, my dilemma: I don't relish being the only swami at Ananda. It seems only natural that my successor should be a swami also. The people I've found, however, who were the most qualified to lead or to instruct others, and whom I've considered also outstanding examples of spirituality—the most unselfish; the most devoted to finding God; the most dedicated to serving Him in others—have been, in almost every case, married.

Years ago, I tried to start a renunciate order at Ananda. The effort failed because the men and women had no choice, in our communitarian way of life, but to mix freely with one another. Now, with the community's growing maturity, it is becoming more feasible to have separate groups within the larger Ananda community. More recently, groups of *brahmacharis* and *brahmacharinis*—men and women renunciates—have been forming. I hope that some of them will in time become swamis.

It has pained me, however, to think of titles in our work being necessarily attached to positions of outer importance. Personally, I have always enjoyed viewing myself as quite *un*important—indeed, as essentially non-existent. My Guru tried to get me to accept, for the work, the rightness of accepting mentally also the positions of prominence he gave me. I myself, however, resisted mental identification with that role. We may say that, in this matter, I was not wholly obedient, but I think obedience itself must be tied to understanding. I did understand the need for the positions he gave me, and tried to fulfill them responsibly. As he himself put it, "In an army, there have to be captains as well as privates." Even so, I always *liked*, and still prefer, to think of myself as insignificant. I found a solution to my dilemma in the recollection that, in any case, God alone is the Doer.

What I've particularly resisted, however, has been the thought of giving anyone a "leg up," institutionally, with what should be only a spiritual title. The simplest answer, I now realize, is to divorce our renunciate order from identity with any outward position.

There is no good reason to suppose that those who hold high positions must necessarily be outstanding in anything but the skills that qualify them for their position. A good leader may in fact not be deeply spiritual. A person's degree of spirituality is for God to decide. In a later chapter I shall discuss institutions and the individual. I've addressed this subject also, over the years, in others of my writings;* it is especially important to right understanding of the spiritual path. Let me continue the thought here, however, of a non-institutional renunciate order.

In institutionalism, as in dogmatism, one encounters many fixed concepts. These include heights above which it is impossible to rise. For instance, in an institution there is no position above that of president, chairman of

---

* See, for example, *God Is for Everyone*, chapter 7, and another book, *Religion in the New Age*.

the board, CEO, or whatever other designation has been given to the top position. Yet most spiritual people have little interest in attaining high posts. Their talents may bring them to such institutional heights, but they have no ambition to achieve those heights. Usually, indeed— or so I suspect—there is an inward pull away from them, particularly since prominence so easily brings with it the temptation of pride.

To preserve the renunciates of this new order from that temptation, I would like to separate the title, Swami, from outward position in any work—that is to say, from *necessary* association with a responsible, leading role. This means that, although a swami may hold such a position, his dedication should be seen by all, including himself, as a primarily spiritual one.

Thus, I can imagine swamis living solitary lives (though perhaps only after some time) in caves or in little *kutirs* (huts). I can also imagine them not even following the path to which I myself have dedicated my life. Since Paramhansa Yogananda was sent, however, to help bring fundamental change to an entire civilization, I must say that I do visualize all swamis of this new renunciate order accepting him as their *adi* (first, or supreme) guru. They needn't at all, however, be members of Ananda, of which I myself am the founder.

The important thing is a person's spirit. The new order I envision is based less on outward rejection of the obvious impediments to enlightenment—desires; worldly attachments; petty self-definitions (such as those pertaining to caste, family background, social status, wealth)—and more on positive attainments, the foremost of which is freedom from ego-consciousness.

I would say that this last, freedom from ego-consciousness, is the primary direction I envision for true renunciation.

It must always be understood that what this renunciate order will emphasize is *direction*, not fixed attainments. Sin itself, my Guru used to say, is only error. People, in their quest for bliss, seek it first in countless mistaken directions. They suffer, try a new direction, fail, then try again. Only after many incarnations do they come to understand that the bliss they've so long been seeking is simply not to be found in mere things, or people, or positions, or worldly fulfillments such as pleasure, power, revenge, fame, or some other of the myriad will-o'-the-wisps mankind seeks. It is to be found only in communion with God. Paramhansa Yogananda used to say, "A saint is a sinner who never gave up [trying, that is to say, to attain oneness with God]."

Fixed rules belong to Kali Yuga. Fixed rules can be (and often are) broken. The true path to God is *directional*; it does not consist of fixed and absolute regulations. The important thing is that one's true direction be upward, not downward: toward God, not away from Him. A slip is not a fall, and does not in any way deserve to be condemned.

I once said to my Guru, "I would rather *die* than succumb to temptation." He remonstrated, "Why be so absolute? If you keep trying, God will never let you down." And he often told people, "God doesn't mind your faults. He minds your indifference."

The path I propose is not absolutist. It is directional. One is fit to be a renunciate at every level, including that of swami, as long as he shows that his heart is firmly dedicated to achieving final perfection.

Chapter Three

Colors

The color orange is traditionally worn by swamis in India. (Actually, and more correctly, the color is *gerua*, which comes from the earth and is that color, with an admixture of iron which produces a sort of reddish brown.) Orange belongs to a part of the spectrum that denotes, specifically, an outwardly directed energy.

Red we think of as suggesting, in its baser associations, the emotions of lust or anger. In its higher associations (cherry red), it suggests cheerfulness. In both cases, one thinks of the color red as signifying an outwardly directed energy.

Orange, which lies between red and yellow in the spectrum, is associated with the color of fire. Orange is appropriate for the fiery will power one needs who wants sternly to reject temptation in all its forms.

Yellow—the color worn by Buddhist monks in Thailand—suggests the sunlight of wisdom; insight; creativity; and impartial acceptance of things as they are. This, too, is an excellent color for monks. Again, however, what yellow lacks is *inwardness*. As the sun's rays shine outwardly upon the earth, so yellow suggests wisdom applied outwardly. It lacks, as well, the softening touch of devotional love.

Green suggests health and happiness, though it can also indicate disturbed emotions (think of its frequent association with envy and jealousy).

Blue suggests calmness, kindness, and an expansive consciousness. Blue should, however, convey warm feeling and should not be, for example, a steely blue. A bright (not dark) royal blue seems to me the perfect shade for expressing the renunciate attitude I have in mind. I've tried to show this color on the cover of this book. When printing a book cover, however, it is difficult to reproduce colors accurately: especially, I am told, the color blue. To see the color more accurately displayed, you can view the book cover on the internet, at www.nayaswami.org.

Indigo and violet—to complete the spectrum, which we might recall to memory by the acronym, Roy G. Biv (some people prefer its opposite: Vibgyor)—are actually the most spiritual colors when thought of as light. Both indigo and violet, however, when seen in dim light, appear almost black.

In Western monasticism, brown, black, or white have been the traditional colors, indicating humility, self-abasement, and (in the case of white) purity of heart. Brown and black in themselves, however, express no joy. The egolessness I want to encourage is joyful, not drab or sorrowful, and not focused on sins and sinfulness.

Yogananda once went to an evangelical meeting in Los Angeles. The minister cried out at one point, "You are all sinners. Get down on your knees!" The Master later reported, "In that gathering of thousands, I was the only one who was not on his knees. I would not admit that I was a sinner!"

It is high time for the Christian emphasis on sin to be transformed into a fresh emphasis on man's potential for perfection in God. As Jesus Christ himself said, "Be ye therefore perfect, even as your Father which is in heaven is perfect." (Matt. 5:48)

24

White is a good renunciate color, for it emphasizes purity of heart, and reminds one, again, of the words of Jesus: "Blessed are the pure in heart: for they shall see God." (Matt. 5:8) White seems to my mind, however, to lack the quality of aspiration which blue can bestow.

My choice, as the best swami color for this Dwapara Age of Energy, is a cheerful, light royal blue.

Why not, one may ask, the traditional orange? Indeed, that color *is* ideal for attitudes of fiery self-control and stern world rejection. It is less ideal, however, for attitudes of devotional soul-expansion. Orange suggests an attitude of authority, which is acceptable if one's first desire is to attain authority and control over himself. It is less acceptable, however, if the color helps to induce an attitude of authority over others, or inclines one to impose his will on them.

In India generally, there has also developed a tendency to treat spiritual authority submissively. Submissiveness is an excellent trait, provided the authority one accepts is rooted in wisdom. It is far from ideal, however, if the teacher himself is lacking in wisdom. We must assume, moreover, that, out of any given number of renunciates even of those who are deeply dedicated to attaining wisdom, not all of them by any means will succeed in that aspiration in this life. Only one who has attained true wisdom is fit to be considered an authority on spiritual matters.

In any case, the divine way always is to *invite*, not to impose. A truly wise person will never impose his wisdom on anyone. He is an authority indeed, yet what he does is *share* what he knows with others— and, moreover, he does so only with those who would listen. How many swamis, by contrast, have I heard declaim their "wisdom" as though exhorting people with untested dogmas!

Thus, even if a swami has true spiritual authority, for him too in these days of widespread skepticism, the color orange may be less appropriate than blue. Orange suggests a need to blast away difficulties, whereas people today are more open to instruction when it is proffered kindly, not forcefully.

Blue, then, both for the renunciate himself and for whatever good he may accomplish in the world, seems the most appropriate color. He should view even teaching as a service and a sharing, not as a declamation of ideas willfully imposed on others.

It is time also, in this age of increasing enlightenment, to emphasize the positive aspects of renunciation: soul-expansion; the inner freedom of simple living; greater mental and spiritual clarity through sexual moderation or, best of all, through complete sexual abstinence; and the sheer delight found by one who has discovered joy in himself.

Orange goes with declamation; blue, with sharing, and with an invitation to others to share.

Orange goes with imposition; blue, with sympathetic self-offering.

Orange, when outwardly directed, can induce egotism. Blue can inspire infinite self-expansion.

Are colors—we must ask finally—all that important? Certainly they are not *all*-important! They do, however, have an influence both subjectively and objectively. It seems wise to cooperate with the natural influences around us, rather than to go counter to them.

Chapter Four

Institutions and the Individual

"God," Sri Yogananda stated, "is center everywhere, circumference nowhere." Other great men of God through the ages, including both Hindus and Christians, have made the same or similar statements. Paramhansa Yogananda gave the institution he founded the name, "Self-Realization Fellowship." The name referred to individual enlightenment. His purpose in conferring this name was not to create a tightly structured organization, with its every directive delivered downward to a submissive and even mindless army of spiritual soldiers.

In training his disciples, Yogananda was careful never to "break" their will. I remember once when I, as a disciple of only a few days, decided to undergo a special fast to purify my body. My Guru, when he learned what I was doing, told me, "It is better to purify the heart." He then told me to continue my fast for one or two days longer—in order, as he put it, not to "break" my will.

How different, this training, from the norm in Western monasteries, where the stated intention is actually to break the neophyte's will, and make him subservient to the Rule and to his "superiors."

It is partly that very word, "superiors," that I challenge in this chapter. Does a person's mere age or seniority in an institution entitle him or her to be considered superior to others? Does high position?

Do even years of training? Yes, certainly, if the training qualifies one to become an example of progress in a particular discipline. But when it comes to spirituality, much more is involved than specific discipline, or even than specific intellectual knowledge.

The search for God takes many incarnations, and not only a few years, or even one lifetime. A person may be born with a level of understanding that is far above that of most people. Shall he submit himself completely to the authority of one who is, himself, still deficient in wisdom? Surely not! Wisdom must reveal itself not by a person's outer raiment or position, but gradually, from within. It cannot be learned as teachings are learned in school, where students graduate and receive their diplomas in batches. Enlightenment is a very personal matter, between each seeker and God.

There is a need for organizations in this world. The human body is itself, in a sense, an organization. Its management is directed downward from the head, and its parts work in harmony under the guidance of that authority. Nations, too, would be fairly chaotic had they no governments to rule them. In this world there is no place for anarchy.

Nevertheless, individual insight is important also; so too is individual conscience, and individual incentive (provided one always respects the rights of others). Unfortunately, in hierarchical institutions, insight, conscience, and incentive are often repressed. (An advocate of such institutions—indeed the woman who threw me out of my Guru's organization—once said to me, "In a corporation, no one has a right *even to think* except the members of the board of directors!" She was, of course, herself on the institution's board of directors. And, later, when I was myself made

28

a director, I found I still had no right to think differently from her.)

Any order of swamis deserving of the name will honor freedom of conscience as a basic ideal. If the swamis belong to an organization—as most of them probably will—the organization itself must honor this ideal. The thought I quoted in the last paragraph, that no one who isn't a board member has any right even to think, belongs to the age of Kali Yuga: centuries of deep intellectual darkness.

The organization I myself have founded, Ananda, holds two tenets particularly sacred: first, *People are more important than things, or than concepts, projects, or even rules*; and the second, *Where there is dharma (right action), there is victory* (the Sanskrit words are, *Yata dharma, sthata jaya*). What we ask of members at Ananda is not mindless obedience, but voluntary, intelligent cooperation.

"Center everywhere, circumference nowhere," though a concept sometimes voiced in Kali Yuga, is far beyond the average kali yugi's comprehension. During that intellectually dark age, people considered that the earth was positioned at the center of whatever universe there was; one's own country was the center of the known world; and one's own self was the center of everything that mattered. During the present Dwapara Yuga, by contrast, people are beginning to reach out toward a greater understanding of the universe.

As far as this process regards renunciation, it is becoming more natural today for people to include the needs of others along with their own; to listen to them more openly, instead of dogmatically declaring their own beliefs. The emphasis, today, is already more on mutual respect. I don't mean the change is radical, but it is at least in the direction of recognizing reality as being less firmly centered in one's own self. Again, the change is directional.

In any age, the essence of spiritual progress is ego-transcendence toward union with Divine Consciousness. In the present age it is easier for people to focus on that purpose directly, instead of approaching it by indirection through non-attachment and strict non-involvement with the material world.

It is easier also, nowadays, to approach that ideal with a positive rather than a negative attitude: by self-expansion, rather than by self-abasement.

Spiritual organizations, then, though excellent in principle, are really worthwhile only if they respect the rights of the individual to his own understanding and individual conscience.

Chapter Five

Samsara vs. Renunciation

Samsara is the world of delusion in which we all live: the cosmic dream. It also signifies emotional involvement with the dream. It was to such emotional involvement that Sri Krishna referred in the advice he gave to Arjuna in the Bhagavad Gita (paraphrased by Paramhansa Yogananda), "O Arjuna! Get away from My ocean of suffering and misery!"

To those few discriminating persons who long to escape from *samsara*, the attempt to overcome outer attachments is an indirect way of extricating oneself from the swamp. A technique I discovered years ago for overcoming attachments was to build a bonfire mentally, and then cast one by one into the flames every attachment of the heart, every like and dislike, every desire.

A woman I know told me recently, "I tried following your advice: In my zeal to overcome attachment to my house, I cast the house itself mentally into a fire. And what happened? The house burned to the ground!" I answered her: "I didn't say to throw the *house* into the fire! What I said was, 'Throw all your *attachments* into it!'"

Even so, overcoming attachments is only an indirect way to inner freedom. In this age of greater enlightenment, it is possible (because at last comprehensible) to work directly on the ego itself, around which all our attachments revolve. Patanjali's definition of yoga, "*Yogas chitta vritti nirodha* (Yoga is the neutralization of the vortices of feeling)," describes the state of true inner freedom. The ego, however, is the eye of that vortex. The ego also rotates in itself, pirouetting constantly in its eagerness for involvement in *maya*.

When the ego has been finally dissolved in cosmic consciousness, pure feeling remains; it is no longer focused, however, or drawn inward to a center, in the little self. One enjoys everything, but without ego-attachment.

The old renunciate method—in itself still valid, however—is negative. It is more uplifting nowadays to concentrate on the positive aspects of renunciation. Burn up all attachments—to home, for instance— but concentrate positively on the complete absence of ego itself. Again, reduce your sense of ego to utter unimportance, but on the other hand concentrate on the joy of freedom in omnipresence. Be humble, but not self-abasing; instead, see God as the true Doer of everything.

The old method of renunciation was world-negating; the new one is *samadhi*-affirming. One's concentration, in other words, is on the joy of soul-freedom in God.

The old renunciate order tended easily toward judgmental attitudes—of others, and (in some ways even worse) excessive judgment of oneself. The new renunciate order concentrates supportively on everyone's soul-potential; it sees all beings as striving, each in his own way, toward union with bliss. This feeling, as it expands outward from one's heart center, beholds that same center of blessing everywhere, in everything, and in everyone. Instead of rejecting error (which of course it must do also; I am not counseling a lack of discrimination!), the new renunciate attitude affirms God's omnipresent bliss.

The new renunciate rises above *samsara* by affirming the divine truth behind everything.

Chapter Six

Men, Women

The Supreme Spirit, as Creator, manifested everything by vibrating what we might call the surface of Its consciousness to produce waves of separate awareness. Where there is vibration, there is duality. This movement of consciousness in opposite directions from a state of rest at the center is what produces Creation.

Duality (*dwaita*) exists everywhere; everything has its own self-canceling opposite. For every joy, there is an equal and opposite sorrow. For every success, there is an equal and opposite failure. Heat is, in the over-all scheme of things, canceled out by cold; pleasure, by pain; light, by darkness; fulfillment, by disappointment; triumph, by disaster. It will be noted that these opposites apply to both mental states and material conditions.

Mankind struggles over countless incarnations to achieve a fulfillment that, out of the very nature of manifested reality, simply cannot but recede before him forever. The sum total of all his striving *must* be zero. (And what a supreme irony: to reflect that the anguished striving of countless incarnations must always end, quite literally, in *nothing*!?)

The dualities are always *equal and opposite*. I have heard men say that women are inferior beings. My monastic superior (a woman) once said to me, "Let's

34

face it, women are more spiritual than men." What nonsense! Men and women are, in every significant sense, equal. In the Ananda communities, no qualitative difference exists between the sexes; both equally have positions of leadership and authority. Nor have I ever observed, in the forty years of Ananda's existence, the slightest spirit of competition between the sexes. A person is judged entirely on the basis of individual merit, never on the basis of gender.

It must be added, however, that just as heat is different from cold, so men and women do differ from each other in the ways they express their essentially divine nature. The position of men's sex organs, being on the outside of their bodies, indicates an energy directed more naturally outward, to the world. Women's organs are inside, an indication of energy directed more inward. Men and women, similarly, differ in their manner of egoic expression. Men are more likely to seek outward conquest. Women's mode of seeking conquest is more likely to be personal, for themselves. Thus, men tend to be impersonal; women, to have a more personal view of things.

I once read of a man who said to a woman friend, "The trouble with women is that they take everything so personally." "Nonsense!" she expostulated. "*I* don't!"

Neither way is better or worse than the other. The two together create, rather, a balance in human nature. Men, as they become more balanced, also grow more sensitive, heartfelt, and concerned for the feelings of others. Women, as their masculine/feminine natures become equalized, develop a more affirmative, impersonal nature, and become more inclined to see life in abstract terms. An Indian woman saint I knew, Ananda Moyi Ma, for whom I felt great devotion, used to say of the Divine Consciousness, "It is and it isn't, and neither is it nor is it not." She was filled as much with wisdom as with love.

Men go more by intellect; women, by feeling. Here again, their very bodies reveal the difference. The male skull is somewhat square, and is often ridged above the eyebrows, indicating an emphasis on reason. Women's foreheads are more rounded, which suggests greater adaptability. Women's breasts are located over the heart region, indicating a more feelingful, and potentially more tender, nature. If their feelings are disturbed, however, women can become intensely (and irrationally) emotional, with all the positive and negative connotations that the word suggests. Men, by contrast, can become too (even absurdly) abstract and analytical. As men's nature becomes balanced, however, they may develop small breasts like those, perhaps, on a thirteen-year-old girl.

The natural attraction between men and women indicates a deeper-than-conscious recognition of their need to balance reason and feeling. The attraction is only secondarily sexual, with the supreme purpose of propagating the species.

Where renunciation is concerned, there must be respect for these differences. There must also be respect, however, for individual variations, which may be great.

Women's renunciation generally ought to help develop in them a caring, nurturing nature. Unfortunately, as one reads in many firsthand accounts, not a few nuns have displayed exceptional lack of feeling toward others, especially toward the children in their care. Their harshness may have come from sexual repression, or it may, in the Catholic Church, come from one-sided emphasis on masculine nature as being the best adapted to religious matters. I have not seen that attitude in the women renunciates at Ananda, though tales about it among Catholic nuns have long puzzled me. One inclines to think the explanation may lie, as I said, in sexual repression.

And I do recall a very different episode in Italy that impressed me: A group of us were seated at an outdoor table in the main piazza at Assisi, drinking coffee. One of our party made a wide gesture while telling a story, and struck the hand of a nun in a white habit just as she was coming up from behind, carrying a cup of espresso coffee. A large brown stain appeared on her all-white habit. Instead of the normal reaction of dismay, she at once smiled and passed off the episode good naturedly. I was well impressed.

So, maybe an attitude of good-humored acceptance is essential—for all renunciates, but for women renunciates perhaps especially.

Humor is certainly a help to men renunciates also. Humorless renunciation can be a grim business. Men ought, I think, to direct their energies particularly toward teaching and a sharing of wisdom. But warm and wise humor can make their very teaching more acceptable.

Men ought to emphasize rather the quest for bliss than for love, lest in love their attitude become too personal. Women, on the other hand, may be drawn more naturally toward developing a loving relationship with God—as Jesus, or Krishna, or Rama. They may be encouraged also to express love in service, in self-giving, and in self-surrender to God.

Men and women renunciates ought, at least for some time on the path, to avoid one another's company as much as possible, or as much as convenient. Only when they can arrive at an impersonal attitude is it somewhat safe for them to mix more freely together.

Even so, they should always be on guard against personal attraction. Sexual attraction, my Guru once said to me, is "the greatest delusion."

Monasteries for men and for women should be kept well apart from one another. The activities of both should be kept separate, too. Men and women renunciates should as much as possible avoid eye contact. And because the sense of touch, of all the senses, is the most involved in sexual desire, it would be wise to avoid hugging others, whether male or female, or even touching each other. The best form of greeting, especially between the sexes, is the Indian *namaskar*, in which one places the palms together respectfully over the heart. Since hugging is so much a part of some cultures, however, I don't forbid people to hug me. I simply don't respond warmly.

Is it (one asks) absolutely necessary—and here I am addressing married persons who want at heart to be renunciates—to forego sex completely? Let us say, rather, that it is extremely helpful. Sexual expression increases ego-consciousness. It also weakens people physically—men especially, but women also lose spiritual strength when their energy moves downward. Moreover, sex not only weakens the will and clouds the mind, but also greatly strengthens the ego. For a person who wants to achieve complete mental clarity, especially in deep meditation, it would be best to forego sex altogether.

Yes, abstinence is the ideal. How many people, however, are able to live by that ideal? Very few! The spiritual path is not a sudden leap to the mountaintop. It is a winding journey to ever-greater heights of freedom, and to ever-more-soaring absorption in God. It is always a help to speak of ideals, but one must also be realistic. In human nature, sex is the second strongest instinct next only to the instinct for self-preservation. Religious teaching must offer people ideals, but it must also suggest ways to *attain* those ideals. Otherwise the teaching itself amounts to little more than blowing breath into a gale.

In the next chapter, this aspect of life will be treated carefully. Here, for now, is a last point: If you are married, follow with everyone the above rules regarding gaze and touch, except for your own spouse, close friends, and relatives.

Chapter Seven

The Main Delusions,
Including the "Greatest" One

I knew a spiritual woman in India who once told me, concerning two well-known and highly respected (but surely not fully Self-realized) saints, "Each of them asked me to have sex with him just once, and promised me spiritual blessings in return. I complied. Imagine my disappointment, then, when I received *no* consequent blessings—not, at least, in the form of any spiritual experience. You can imagine how badly I felt!"

A strange story. Yet I vouch for that person's integrity. Moreover, she had nothing to gain by lying to me. Though she took me into her confidence on this point, there was no hint of any intimacy between the two of us.

I am also inclined to believe that she probably did get good karma for helping those men toward final freedom from desire, though I fault them for not being completely truthful with her. Well, I am not in a position to judge, and I do appreciate their difficulty. To abstain from sex totally is very difficult, and can result, as Sigmund Freud said, in serious complexes. I myself, as far as I can tell, have attained freedom from this basic instinct, but it was only by the special grace of God, and not by any virtue of my own. All I could do, until then, was try. God and Guru gave me this inner freedom. And I must say with perfect truthfulness that I had to undergo much suffering to attain this condition.

For most people, marriage is the safest route. Loyalty

to one person can remove the temptation to seek a multiplicity of sexual adventures. Moderation, ending in complete abstinence, is much easier for most people than to abstain immediately and completely.

The trouble with marriage is that it tends to separate people in other ways also from a feeling of universal sympathy for everyone. It may close people off in fenced enclosures of likes and dislikes. Marriage is certainly best avoided for those who want to give their hearts entirely to God. But one must also ask himself realistically, "What am I capable of doing?" There are people who marry out of the pure thought that they will be better able to serve God in the married state. Such people are blessed—if, indeed, they succeed.

My Guru told us of a saint he had met as a young man. "Are you married?" the saint inquired of him. "No," Master replied.

"You are on the safe side," the saint told him. "I myself am married, and my wife is very materialistic. Still, I have escaped her at last: She doesn't know where I am!" My Guru explained that his escape had been into the inner Self.

In another story told me by my Guru, he said a young married friend of his had once confessed to him, "I used to have many friends, and I enjoyed their company. But now that I am married I find I don't seek them out anymore. My friendship with them was in fact only a subconscious longing for the fulfillment of a mate."

"Thank you very much!" my Guru replied. "You have taught me something important."

"Since then," he continued, "I have always maintained a little distance from others."

In marriage, especially for couples who are seeking God-communion together, there a natural tendency to seek intimacy on an increasingly spiritual level. My Guru's parents came together as man and wife only once a year, for the purpose of having children. Once a year may be too difficult for most people, but—once a month? That, certainly, is better than once a week. And couples who come together sexually several times a week may as well prepare their coffins and keep them in readiness for that last gasp! For if they don't die physically, they will certainly be courting spiritual death—like those people Jesus Christ described when he said, "Let the dead bury their dead." (Matt. 8:22) By too-frequent sex, in other words, people lose that refinement which lifts mankind above the dumb beasts.

Even in sex, one's attitude should be more self-giving than of wanting personal pleasure. The physical act should be an expression above all of love; it should not be undertaken for mere excitement.

Is the single state of *brahmacharya* better? It depends on the individual. I have known married people who were more dedicated to God than most renunciates. Total renunciation often induces pride, which, in itself, is an enormous obstacle on the path. On the other hand—as St. Paul said—a married person thinks more about his wife and how he can please her. A renunciate thinks, "How can I best please God?"

My Guru actually wrote in *Autobiography of a Yogi*, "To fulfill one's earthly responsibilities is indeed the higher path, provided the yogi, maintaining a mental uninvolvement with egotistical desires, plays his part as a willing instrument of God."*

During Kali Yuga, it was almost always necessary to renounce the world if one wanted to know God. Lahiri Mahasaya, however, in this new Dwapara Yuga, voluntarily undertook the dharma of a householder to

---

* p. 222, first edition reprint, Crystal Clarity Publishers.

42

show people that human understanding has evolved to the point where it is possible even in the married state to find God.

In the new renunciate order I am proposing, one may work toward becoming, and in fact may actually be, a swami even if he is married. Couples may work together toward that goal. It depends first of all on how earnestly they want to transcend ego-consciousness, and to follow the other conditions which I mentioned at the end of Chapter 1. More is involved in such transcendence, however, than sexual self-control. The other main delusions include the desire for, and attachment to, possessions, pleasures, and money. Couples, in their very anxiety to please each other, may be more attached to that delusive satisfaction than are single individuals. A husband may want to buy his wife jewels or other ego-pleasing items that he would never think of getting for himself. A wife may want to provide a nice home for her husband even if she might never have had such an interest for herself.

If a person wants to transcend ego-consciousness, he should learn to accept slights and insults calmly and impersonally. If he or she is married, however, it is much more difficult to remain calm if one's spouse is insulted.

One may feel no pride, personally, but it is very difficult not to feel proud of the appearance, ability, or success of one's spouse.

In fact, it is more difficult to overcome the sense of "I" and "mine" when one is emotionally linked to someone else.

The fact that such liberating attitudes are more difficult to acquire in the married state, however, makes the victory, once it is achieved, all the greater. Ideally, one should tell himself, "All this belongs to God." If one's mate is shown disrespect or is insulted, one should certainly be loyal to that person as one's own, but he need not let himself be upset. Calmness under all circumstances is right and good. To return insult for insult is a sign of spiritual immaturity. It is not an insult, however, to reply, "Your opinion tells me more about who and what you are than about my wife/husband. To concentrate on the faults in one who is trying to become good is ignoble." One might add, then, "Well, I prefer to see the God in you than to concentrate on the ignorance." This might be a sharp reply, but no spiritual teaching says one should become a doormat for others.

In creating a beautiful home, think of making it a place of peace and harmony, not a showcase for the admiration (and perhaps envy!) of others. Usually, more happiness is found in simplicity than in elaborate display. See that you and your spouse live above all for God, and don't concern yourselves with the good opinion of others. In developing this attitude together, there comes a certain happiness that single renunciates seldom know. A clear conscience, when shared with another person, brings with it satisfaction of a very special kind.

Indeed, God did not make this universe for us to abhor it. He is pleased when we enjoy things *with His joy.* And He certainly is pleased when we can share our enjoyment with others.

As far as income is concerned, it is certainly easier for an unmarried renunciate to refuse a salary, and to leave his security entirely in the hands of God. For a married person, even if he is a renunciate at heart, he would show irresponsibility if he cared nothing about income or security. He has a duty to his spouse (and to his family, if he has one), and cannot ask them to accept such extreme non-attachment as Jesus

Christ showed in saying, "Take no thought for your life, what ye shall eat, or what ye shall drink; nor yet for your body, what ye shall put on. Is not the life more than meat, and the body than raiment?" (Matt. 6:25) Here and elsewhere, Jesus taught an extreme form of renunciation that would not be practicable for the average person, and particularly not for the householder. Yet complete nonattachment can be achieved also by giving generously of one's worldly goods to others; by using what goods one has to help others; and by offering those goods in service to God. In this sense, those who fulfill their earthly duties with an attitude of generous concern for the well-being of others may develop faster, spiritually, than those who, being accustomed to living on charity, develop an attitude of receiving, not of giving. Those who have nothing material to give others must concentrate all the more on sharing their spiritual wealth with others.

In every case, the important thing is ego-transcendence. All blessings come from God. To the true renunciate, whatever comes, whether fulfillment or deprivation, is a sign of divine grace. One must be forever grateful to God for the lessons he receives. And he must always share, in token of that gratitude, whatever blessings he is given in life.

If, in confrontation with any of the great delusions, one finds himself slipping downhill, he should never blame himself or say, "I have failed!" If he keeps on trying, he will justify the words Paramhansa Yogananda uttered, which I quoted earlier: "A saint is a sinner who never gave up." Instead of blaming oneself, one should mentally resist delusion (even if, in weakness, he momentarily succumbs to it). He should always affirm, "I will climb out of this pit of delusion eventually, no matter how many times I fail, for it is not *my* delusion.

It is only Satan's power active within me. I *will* conquer in the end, for I am not a child of Satan, but of God. I *will* find freedom in Divine Bliss, eventually!"

One should never, of course, use this teaching as an excuse to err, for delusion is very subtle, and *maya* uses every rationalization to trap the unwary. If one can't help oneself, however, he should never despair. As Krishna says in the Bhagavad Gita, "Even the worst of sinners can, with the raft of wisdom, cross safely over the ocean of delusion." (4:36)

Periods of preparation should be required of all those who want to take any serious step. Those who are not yet ready to become *brahmacharis* (single renunciates who have committed not to marry) or *tyagis* (married renunciates)—perhaps because of uncertainty as to whether or not they want someday to become married, or perhaps because they have children who are under eighteen—may embrace vows as pilgrims, signifying their sincere dedication to finding God. This may be considered also a period of postulancy, the length of time before embracing brahmacharya or tyaga to be determined by time and experience.

Let me try, finally, to sum up the benefits of the married versus the single state for those who seek to become true renunciates:

Advantages of the Married State

1. Marriage helps those so inclined to equalize their own feminine and masculine natures. Each can learn from the other attitudes that contribute to the complete human being.

2. Marriage makes it easier, for one so inclined, to bring sexual desire under control. With a single partner, novelty and excitement often disappear,

46

if only gradually. Constant availability reduces the sense of adventure. And while it makes sex easy and convenient for those who want to enjoy it, it also, for those who desire transcendence, renders it easier to avoid.

3. Marriage makes—or can make—it easier to free the mind from obsession with sex, and to focus on loftier realities.

4. Commitment to the married state helps to protect one from the sexual predators of this world, whether at the office or anywhere else. A wedding ring helps both men and women to make the unspoken statement, "I am not available."

5. Each partner in a marriage can help the other to appreciate and adopt a more balanced point of view. The woman may help the man to see things and people more intuitively. The husband may help his wife to become less emotionally attached, and to see things more clearly from a point of view of duty.

6. Each member of a marriage partnership can strengthen the other in facing the world and dealing with it.

7. Marriage can be self-expansive. In concern for someone besides oneself it becomes easier to reach out to others, and, in time, to the whole world. In the Hindu religion, the wife is taught to love the husband not for his own sake only, but as God in that form. And the husband, similarly, is taught to love his wife as an expression of the Divine Mother.

Disadvantages of the Married State

1. The married state is spiritually disadvantageous if it encourages an attitude of what my Guru called, "Us four and no more." It can create a sort of closed corporation before which the needs of others become either secondary or nonexistent.

2. The married state can easily produce satisfaction with mediocrity. In this case, it kills all high spiritual aspiration.

3. The married state easily tempts one to think, first, "How can I please my spouse," rather than, "How can I best please God?"

4. Marriage draws one more easily into a social milieu. Couples meet together often, and chat endlessly about things that, to the true devotee, seem almost appallingly trivial.

5. Marriage could be self-expansive, but usually it is self-confining in the sense that it limits people to homely concerns, to children and *their* concerns, and to social gossip.

6. Marriage emphasizes the commonplace, and makes it more difficult to develop one-pointed devotion to God.

7. Marriage, when it is not a true partnership, can easily induce a sense of competition, one with the other. Disharmony can result, and awaken mutually harmful emotions.

8. Marriage requires a lot of energy, devoted to keeping the relationship healthy and vibrant. And if one adds children to the mix, the amount of time and energy multiplies exponentially. While these areas of life don't necessarily pull one away

48

from the spiritual life, they often do so simply by limiting the amount and quality of any service one might render beyond the home.

9. A married person is not always free to follow his conscience. My Guru said, "We used to have couples living in Encinitas, but I found that, if perchance I scolded one, the other would always spring to that spouse's defense."

10. One is much more likely, if married, to develop such negative emotions as jealousy, anger, and displeasure.

Advantages of the Single State

1. The single person is free to please God above all, to think of Him, to talk to Him mentally, and to follow purely and unobstructedly, and with fewer objections from others, the path of *dharma* (spiritual duty).

2. The single man is saved from the danger of having a nagging wife. And the single woman is saved from the equally pernicious danger of finding herself saddled with a domineering husband. The man usually is physically stronger, but, as my Guru often pointed out, "A woman with a six-inch tongue can kill a man six feet tall!"

3. If the single person wants to achieve sexual self-control, he will find it easier—other things being equal—not to have a partner constantly beside him or her, making sexual advances and demands.

4. It is much easier for a single person to develop an impersonal attitude toward life and toward others. He is less inclined to think of his own needs, and tends to focus rather on serving humanity.

5. A single person can more easily develop such spiritual attitudes as the thought, "What comes of itself, let it come." He therefore finds it easier to escape the ensnaring meshes of past karma.

6. It is easier for a single person to escape ego-consciousness. Marriage demands constant interaction with others, and may destroy, therefore, all chance of affirming mentally, "I, as an individual, don't really even exist."

7. Single people can more easily open their hearts to the needs of others, and serve them selflessly. It is more difficult for married people to banish personal motives from their hearts, and to think only in terms of doing what is right.

8. Austerity—a measure of which is necessary in all true renunciation—is easier to practice for one who is single, and whose fate is not linked to that of another human being.

9. It is much easier, in the single state, to practice inner and outer silence.

10. It is much easier, if one is single, to adopt new directions in life, as one feels inwardly directed.

11. It is easier to remain even-minded when one has no one else's moods or interests to contend with.

12. It is easier, finally, to see God always as the Doer when there isn't someone around always asking, "Why did you do that? What do you plan to do about . . . ? You are always so . . . !" In fact, marriage itself would be a great deal happier if that single word, "always," were rigidly excluded from every conversation!

Disadvantages of the Single State

1. Single people can more easily become one-sided, imagining the masculine or the feminine view to be the only realistic one.

2. Single people incline more easily toward eccentricity, instead of finding their true center in themselves.

3. Single people who refrain from marriage against their own natural inclination may develop distorted personalities—exaggerated harshness, for example, or intolerance of others. These attitudes are often, I believe, symptoms of sexual repression.

4. Single people more easily become selfish, inconsiderate of others, and self-indulgent.

5. Single people may take themselves too seriously—more so than people who are married.

Those Who, Though Married, Want to Seek God on Their Own

It sometimes happens that divine yearning awakens in one's heart *after* he has committed himself to the married state. If this desire includes a strong impulse to live alone, the following thoughts should be kept in mind:

1. One has already made a serious commitment. He or she now has another person to consider in any such radical decision. If one's spouse is worldly, selfish, foolish, or opposed to the spiritual search, one is free to consider the spiritual dictum: "If a duty conflicts with a higher duty, it ceases to be a duty." If, however,

one's spouse sincerely wants to join him in his quest for God, he must honor that desire and not renounce him/her.

2. If the other person, though sincere and good, wants to draw him (or her) away from a life of spiritual dedication, the higher duty is to separate.

3. If one has the consent of one's spouse, one is free to dissolve the marriage contract.

I may conclude by saying that I myself prefer the single state, though I should also add that I did, for a time, embrace marriage. My purpose in doing so was to show the members of our Ananda community that God can be sought sincerely, whether one is single or married. After a few years I was released from that obligation, and returned happily to my norm: the single state. I bear my former wife only good will, but my life truly was meant to be lived for God alone.

Chapter Eight

A Step at a Time

Paramhansa Yogananda, when a boy, had a vision in which he saw himself standing in the dusty marketplace of a Himalayan village. The scene around him roiled with the noise of people, confusion, the turmoil of conflicting ambitions and desires, and the urgency of self-interest. Dogs ran everywhere. Monkeys clambered down from roofs to snatch at food from the stalls. People protested loudly at whatever prices they were offered.

Every now and then someone would pause before young Mukunda (as he was then known) and gaze at a spot somewhere behind him. A look of inexpressible yearning would come over that person's face. Then he would turn away again, and mutter sorrowfully, "Oh, but it's much too high for me!" That person would then turn back again to the hot, dusty marketplace and reassume his link with the world around him.

The same thing happened several times. At last, young Mukunda turned around to see what had awakened such deep longing in those few people. There behind him he beheld a high mountain, at the top of which he saw, spread out invitingly, a large, enchantingly beautiful garden. What a thrilling contrast it made to the heat, the noise, the dirt, the confusion in the busy village around him!

His first thought was what those persons had expressed: "Oh, but it's much too high for me!" But then came a sterner thought: "Well, I can at least put one foot in front of the other!" Armed with determination, he set out to climb the mountain. The trek took a long time, but at last he arrived at, and joyfully entered into the paradise garden at the top.

Who would not greatly prefer to live free from pain or sorrow, in perfect happiness or even bliss? Alas, people dread the effort it would take. They consider themselves unworthy, or unfit, or incapable, or too steeped in worldliness. They cannot even imagine themselves inwardly free. Yet there are a few who *yearn* to escape from this snake pit of delusion. They've suffered enough here on earth, and have realized at last that there simply is no way to find the release they seek, except in God. Thus, they gaze yearningly, at last, at the heights of spiritual attainment.

How splendid it would be if God's love alone could attract us! Nearly all suffering, alas, is a necessary prod toward the spiritual heights. Faintheartedness, for a time, causes one's courage to fail: those divine attainments seem "much too high!" At last only, as the soul's determination grows gradually more firm, one sets forth up the long trail, putting one foot in front of the other. Those who never give up arrive finally at the top.

In every generation, a few determined and undeterrable souls do complete the journey.

What, then, are the stages on the journey? It is easy to refer to them vaguely, but in fact they constitute an endless series of little, separate, and even specific acts of will.

With sex, for instance, my Guru told me, "The first thought: *that* is the moment to catch it."

Our very thoughts, he said, do not originate in ourselves, but emanate from various levels of consciousness. "Thoughts are universally and not individually rooted" was how he expressed it in *Autobiography of a Yogi*. That "first thought" represents a direction of one's attention toward some universal influence, whether it be toward deeper involvement in delusion, or toward self-mastery. If our first thought is of God, or of self-control, divine grace will enter our minds and will influence us. But if that thought opens mental windows onto scenes of desire, we may tell ourselves complacently (because that desire may still be only slight), "Never mind, I will be all right." In this thought, however, we will fail to take into account the fact that any thought, if indulged in, will open the mind to the cosmic influences pertaining to that particular level of consciousness.

Divine grace itself is like the sunlight on the side of a building. If we open wide to that light the curtains in our room, the light will enter and flood us with warmth. But if we keep our mental curtains closed— or, to strain the image only a little—if we *entertain* wrong thoughts (*entertain* being the right word in this case!) satanic influence will enter our minds, and will try to influence us further in a direction that we may not at first have desired at all.

By gazing, the Bhagavad Gita states, attraction develops; from attraction comes desire; desire (when thwarted) awakens anger; from anger comes delusion; from delusion comes confusion regarding what is right or wrong; and from mental confusion comes complete absorption in the particular delusion concerned.

Shopkeepers in India say to their customers, "Looking is free!" Delusion, too, insinuates the idea, "Thinking is free!" Don't you believe it! When the first thought of delusion in *any* form enters the mind, direct your attention vigorously elsewhere.

If someone of the other sex seems to you especially attractive, immediately withdraw your energy from that thought, and then impersonalize it: perhaps by thinking of the beauties in Nature everywhere. Don't try to change the attraction into repulsion, for repulsion is only the other side of the coin from attraction, and can easily swing back again to its first manifestation. You may find it helpful, however, to imagine that person some fifty years from now! or to imagine him/her in an angry or a vindictive mood.

Then look away; don't feast your gaze on outer appearance. Remember, much suffering follows from emotional involvement of any kind. Keep your ego free—free above all to enjoy God's love and bliss.

Avoid physical contact of any kind, even a light touch of the arms, hands, or fingers.

Put yourself in a proactive mode, not a receptive one. Think and speak forcefully about something about which your feelings are impersonal. Be impersonal not only toward the other person, but also toward yourself.

When I was in college, a certain girl in our little circle of friends kept hinting that she'd like me to take her out on a date. Finally I did ask her out. When I brought her back to her dormitory, she exclaimed fervently, "You are so *wonderful!*" Immediately the thought arose in my mind, "Anyone so lacking in discrimination would surely be best avoided!" I never took her out again, though we remained "coffee table" friends.

It will help you very much mentally to reject any flattery you receive from others.

When you see beauty, or charm, or any other attractive quality in another person, don't imagine you will absorb that quality into yourself by physically embracing him, or her! Differentiate the quality itself from the person manifesting it; try to think of it as a quality you too can develop in yourself. *Emulate* it; don't try to possess it as if squeezing toothpaste out of a tube. Remember, the beauty of the clouds at sunset is due only to the animating light of the sun.

If, driven by delusion, you find yourself impelled toward personal involvement with someone, mentally resist that thought even if in fact you succumb to the temptation.

Refuse to make a big thing of any delusion. Take no one's judgment of you to heart. People judge others for those faults about which they themselves feel guilty. Tell yourself, then, "Even if I am still weak, my true happiness will never lie in this direction. It is therefore not the way I choose to go." Sometimes a fisherman must let a fish swim free with the bait for a time, as the best way of eventually pulling it in. To pull on the line too determinedly may only break it. You *are not* your mistakes. Why, then, exaggerate them to the point where you break the lifeline of self-control?

Don't criticize, resent, or hate anyone who tries to tempt you. Don't give that person so much power over you! The best reaction, often, is a free and merry (but not a mocking) laugh; then direct your attention elsewhere.

A story might be helpful here from the years I spent with my Guru; it is one I don't think I have told before. A famous Hollywood movie actress once visited and lunched with him. I served the meal, and afterward sat in the room to record their conversation. At one point she exclaimed with great enthusiasm, "I *love* sex!" I was amused, but Master, after her departure, commented with an expression of disgust, "She is a demon!"

If you find it difficult to withdraw from a special attraction to any one person, diffuse that feeling by directing it broadly toward everyone else around you.

Watch for two things in yourself: First, a feeling of excitement in your heart when in the presence of any particular person of the other sex—and indeed generally, when in the company of all persons of the other sex. This feeling can be awakened in people of all ages. A lady of my acquaintance once said to me, "My little daughter, aged three, has a special giggle she affects only in the company of little boys."

Second, watch for the slightest stirring or stimulation of energy in the second *chakra*, or spinal plexus. The nerves from this center go out to the sex organs. Excited energy, whether in the *chakra* or in the organs themselves, is a danger signal. It may be too subtle for immediate awareness, but watch for the symptoms.

Men should think of women generally in their nurturing and self-giving aspect—as mothers, perhaps, or as sisters, and not as ego-attracting temptresses or as a temptation in themselves. The energy women themselves put out should be impersonal, not provocative.

Women should regard men as ideal fathers or brothers, or as potential teachers or guides. Generally, they should maintain a slight, respectful distance. It will not help them, in themselves, to treat men condescendingly, competitively, or with predatory gaze.

Nor should men regard women with a predatory gaze. It is the masculine nature to give energy. Feminine nature tries to draw energy from the masculine. Both sexes should see to it that the giving, as well as the attracting, is of the highest order, directed from the higher *chakras* in the spine, or—best of all—from the Christ center between the eyebrows. Both should try to see people in their genderless souls.

I have concentrated on sex here simply because it is, as my Guru said, "the greatest delusion." The same

58

methods can be used, however, for virtually any delusion that threatens to take one from his inner center.

Above all, please remember the saying, "Rome was not built in a day." Seek freedom gradually, one step at a time. This applies to the overcoming of every delusion. *"Banat, banat, ban jai!"* was the advice Lahiri Mahasaya gave his disciples: Doing a little bit daily, one step at a time, one finds himself at last on the spiritual summit.

Chapter Nine

Transcending the Ego

In all delusions, finally, the feelings that accompany them revolve around the ego. When you want something even as insignificant as an ice cream cone, the thought in your mind is, "*I* want it; it's for *me*; I will get to enjoy it *myself!*" This is what I mean by revolving one's feelings around the ego. They verily "churn" the ether.

Our first need, then, is to neutralize those feelings: our emotional reactions; our likes and dislikes; our attractions and aversions; our attachments and repulsions. Hence Patanjali's definition of yoga as *chitta vritti nirodha*—the neutralization of the vortices of feeling.

Our subtlest and most intimate feelings, however, pertain directly to the ego itself, and act as constant ego-reminders: ego-boosters, ego-deflators. These tendencies must be completely eliminated before we can achieve liberation. Each vortex of feeling draws energy inward to its center in egoic awareness. The ego itself forms the supreme vortex.

In the simple thought, "I want an ice cream cone," two concepts exist: "I," and "ice cream cone." The concept "I" ties the ice cream cone to oneself, but if I emphasize that thought further and think, "How clever of me to have had this idea!" And then, "How much more clever than my friends, who thought only of drinking a glass of water!" And then maybe even,

"It's people like me who help to boost the national economy!" And finally, "They ought to make *me* the next president!" In all this we see that the ice cream cone itself has come to play a minor role compared to the more central thought, "I."

When the thought of self becomes paramount, the ego takes to spinning about itself, becoming ever larger as it does so. It is good to work on eliminating all desires, but it is even more important to do one's best to diminish the magnetic power of the ego itself, for the greater that magnetism, the greater also will be the number of outer fulfillments it will attract to itself.

It is necessary above all, therefore, to attack ego-consciousness directly, and not only to work indirectly at removing, one by one, every outward attachment and desire. If I want fame, for instance, it is more important to convince myself of my own unimportance than to become merely convinced of the shallowness of public recognition. If I want money, it is important to persuade myself that the self-glorification induced by wealth is worse than attachment to a swollen bank account.

Paramhansa Yogananda used to say, "Money and fame are like prostitutes: loyal to no man." Yet the pride they induce are like a disease which eats directly at one's inner peace and happiness. A person may rightly say that if one takes advantage of others, he will live in constant fear of being taken advantage of in return. In himself, however, the self-affirmation that accompanies such wrong behavior is a ball and chain heavier and more self-impeding than attraction to the desired objects themselves. If I steal, I affirm my own worth as a human being above that of other human beings. If I seek fame for myself rather than for whatever good I may be able to accomplish in the world, I push my ego above all the other waves around me, and try, as a result, to distance myself from my own true source in God.

Thus, more important than working on specific desires, attachments, and outwardly directed delusions is the work I do to eliminate my sense of separateness from the great Ocean of Life.

What can I do, then, to minimize this supreme self-definition—this unceasing awareness that I am in some way separate and different from everything and everyone else? Here are a few suggestions:

1. When someone tells a good story, don't try to "top" it with another one. Let his story receive the appreciation it deserves. Laugh appreciatively. Be generous: allow him this moment in the limelight.

2. When someone praises you, consider (before you respond) whether even a modest disclaimer of worthiness may not make you appear to be slighting his opinion, or his good taste. If, for example, someone compliments you on how nicely you are dressed, don't reply with a deprecating laugh, "What, these old rags!?" It would be far better simply to thank him. Or again, if he compliments you for something you've done, answer him, "Thank you, though your praise belongs to God, who alone is the true Doer."

3. When someone has a good idea, even one you yourself have already had, you may find it helpful to say simply, "That's a good idea!" Don't say, "Yes, I've often had that same thought myself."

4. If someone makes an incorrect statement, don't bother to correct him—unless you consider it important to do so. But if it does seem important

enough to speak up, then, instead of flatly con-
tradicting him, make it clear first that you know
he is interested only, as are you, in the trutvh.

5. When someone tells a joke, don't tell another
one unless you think it will add to the conversation. Don't speak, in other words, merely to be
heard, or out of a wish to "top" him.

6. Don't be self-effacing. Simply show calm respect
to everyone. Show respect even to foolish people—and more so, if anything, to children, because of the common tendency to speak to them
condescendingly. The children may be wiser
than you think. But I have found that even foolish people may sometimes be used by God to
keep one humble.

7. In conversation, don't wait impatiently for your
"chance to speak your piece." Listen respectfully, and, if possible, listen with interest. Try
to make it a *conversation*, not a competition of
monologues.

8. Be sincere. Don't "back bashfully into the limelight"—as someone once described Albert Ein-
stein doing. Let your modesty express your true
feeling, and not be a show you put on to impress
others. Persuade yourself by countless and constant little affirmations that you are only a ripple
on the great Ocean of Consciousness. Only the
Divine Ocean itself is of any true consequence.

9. In group conversations, be neither a groundhog
(diving into your hole in fear of your own shadow) nor a lion (beating everyone into submission
with the loudness of your roar), but think rather
in terms simply of sharing with others.

10. When speaking in public, think more in terms of what you share with others than of their impression of you.

11. Show respect for all, but don't insist that they respect you properly. And if they do scorn or insult you, remind yourself, "This is their problem, not mine."

12. Show others appreciation not only because they will then be more likely to appreciate you, but also, and more importantly, because thereby you will expand your own sense of identity.

13. Laugh *with* others, but never *at* them.

14. When someone criticizes you, analyze yourself to see whether there may not be something in you that needs correction. Don't answer hotly or challengingly, "Oh? And what about *you*?!"—proceeding then to list his shortcomings, which balance your own. Don't be defensive, and never try to justify yourself. Often, however, it is a mistake to admit to a fault, for unless the other person is a true friend, he may someday hold that admission over your head. Simply say, "Thank you. Maybe you are right. I will give the matter my careful consideration." In this way you will not involve yourself in any personal or emotional complications.

15. Be more aware of what you give out to others than of what you receive from them. Even in gratitude your focus should be more on your expression of it than on the appreciation you feel. (I am aware that this advice can be twisted, for the good others do to us is *in itself* worthwhile, and in no way depends on our reaction

to it. When I was a small child, I once said to my mother, "So-and-so gave me a candy, and I said, 'Thank you.' Wasn't that good of me?" Mother replied, "No, it wasn't good. It was what you *should* have done!" Good advice, indeed! Never bask in your own glory. Do good to others, then forget it. The good that you do belongs to the universe. Why limit it by centering it in yourself?)

16. If someone calls you a fool, say, "Thank you. I like to be reminded of how unimportant I really am."

17. If someone calls you a genius, say, "Thank you. Though I do my best, I am well aware that any good I do comes not from me, but from God. The beauty of the clouds at sunset is due only to the sun's light upon them."

18. If someone belittles something you've done, say to him, "I am sorry it doesn't please you. I hope to succeed better next time." Meanwhile, tell yourself, "The fruits of all my actions, whether good, mediocre, or bad, belong only to God. It is He who has dreamed this whole show."

19. If someone laughs at you, try sincerely to laugh with him. If he tells a story about you that makes you look ridiculous, again, laugh with him—and then, if you like, tell another one on yourself in the same vein. Do this with a view above all of deflecting from yourself any thought that may arise in your mind that you deserve better treatment. If, however, his laughter is deliberately unkind, inappropriate, or in bad taste, calmly show your lack of interest, and divert the conversation to another topic.

20. If a shopkeeper quotes you a price that seems to you outrageous for something you want to buy, don't rail at him. Say instead, "I'm sure it's worth that price to you, but it's more than I myself will pay." Show him respect, in other words; don't haggle with him, or say disgustedly, "What, *that* price for such a piece of junk?" (After all, you've already shown your own interest in that "junk.") Secondly, by showing him that you respect him, you'll receive from him the best price possible, for he'll want to show you respect in return. For yourself, moreover— and this is our present concern—you won't create waves of reaction that would inevitably return at last to yourself.

21. In competition against others—in sports, for instance—do your best to win, but tell yourself you are really competing against yourself, to improve your own skill. Whether you win or lose, be gracious. I remember once, when I was sixteen, that I was losing a tennis game against someone whom I considered an inferior player to myself. To "teach him a lesson," I gave the ball a vicious uppercut with my racket—thereby demonstrating the worst possible form in that game! (One is supposed to hold the racket parallel to the ground.) I hit myself on the nose with the racket, and caused it to bleed heavily. In fact, I broke my nose. I remember lying there on the court, laughing heartily at the absurdity of my own action, which had so thoroughly disproved my high opinion of my own ability. My laughter was for the beauty of this perfect lesson.

22. Never draw people's attention to yourself. Try to keep it centered in the topic under discussion.

23. If someone challenges your point of view, never let the discussion sink to a level of personal animosity. I once mentioned to my father something I'd read once about a claim that the Mexican central plateau had risen suddenly, in a cataclysm, to its present height. My father, who as a geologist believed in what is called "gradualism," scoffed at this claim. When I tried to defend it, he said, "I think you ought to respect my opinion." I replied, "I do indeed respect it—as an opinion." Both of us quickly veered away from what threatened to become a perfectly useless argument.

24. Try to have neither a superiority nor an inferiority complex. Tell yourself simply, "Whatever is, *is*; and whatever I am, I am. I refuse to make value judgments in the matter. All of us are simply playing our parts in the cosmic drama. Let me do my best, only, to play my part well."

25. Every day, and throughout the day, try to reduce your self-definition to zero. If you are famous in the eyes of the world, tell yourself, "I am nothing and no one." If you hold an important position of any kind, tell yourself, "When I die, all this will be lost. Even now, then, I am nothing." If you are unknown, or despised and rejected by others, tell yourself, "In my nothingness, I am *everything*! I am not this body: I am a part—equally so to all other parts—of Infinite Reality!"

26. Try to see God in all, and to love Him in all. For everyone on earth, each in his own way and no matter how mistakenly, is trying to find his own nature: Divine Bliss!

27. When death itself comes—as it must someday—
offer your life up gladly to God: to Infinite Consciousness. Never dwell on the mistakes you've
made in your life. Offer them rather to God, and
tell Him, "I claim for myself no credit or blame for
anything I have done. I am forever an offshoot of
Thy Infinite Perfection."

I have offered here a few suggestions, only, for how
you can rise above ego. Think of these thoughts as
"starters," merely, to guide you in your own efforts to
thread your way through the intricate maze of *maya*.

I remember, years ago, working earnestly on developing humility. To my astonishment I awoke one
morning to the realization that I was becoming proud
of my humility!

Ego-transcendence is the very essence of spiritual
progress. One wonders why so little teaching has been
devoted to it, and so much more emphasis has been
placed on ego-suppression. One wonders also why,
especially among renunciates, so much attention has
been given to indirect efforts such as eliminating attachments and desires. Naturally these self-limitations
must be renounced also, the energy formerly committed to them channeled upward unidirectionally to the
brain and the spiritual eye between the eyebrows. I can
only think that the reason ego-transcendence has received so little attention is that most people during Kali
Yuga could not comprehend that the ego really has no
existence except in its fleeting dream-reality. This brief
seeming is only (as my Guru said) like a glimmer of
sunlight reflected in a sliver of glass on the roadside.

Even at the beginning of this *Dwapara Yuga*, matter itself has been shown to consist only of vibrations
of energy. It is possible, now, to understand at least

intellectually that our separate reality is only an ever-changing cloud, and that we are all, in truth, but a single reality.

Does it look to you as though I were trying to reduce everyone to a pale shadow? If so, let me say further that I myself only really began to accomplish anything in my own life once I'd succeeded in persuading myself that God alone was the Doer.

I tried at one point to see if, by sitting back and turning it all over to Him, He would take over. It was an experiment, nothing more. I was lecturing in church, and at a certain point simply stopped speaking and waited for Him to step in and speak through me.

Well, He didn't. I was convinced, then, that I had to do my bit. Paramhansa Yogananda taught people to pray, "I will reason, I will will, I will act, but guide Thou my reason, will, and activity to the right path in everything."

We have to play our part, but if we tell ourselves, "He is the Doer; He can infuse His power into me," we find He won't do it. At least, as long as I remained unspeaking, complete silence reigned. I was unembarrassed, but some people in the audience believed, anxiously, that I'd frozen with fear.

One or two friends, after reading what I've written about eliminating the ego, have protested, "But how, then, will Master's prediction be fulfilled, when he said, 'Someday lion-like swamis will come from India and spread this message all over'?"

Do they think I've counseled everyone to become a *wimp*? Far from it! The more one can get himself out of the way, the better God will be able to work through him. What happens is that one learns to use his own, but *God-given*, power.

Chapter Ten

Truthfulness

In India I once met a wealthy man who boasted of being a true renunciate. "I have willed all my property," he told me proudly, "to my children. Personally, I own nothing. I am free!"

Yet his self-definition exuded wealth and the pride that accompanies wealth. His "renunciation" was a pure sham (if a sham may be called "pure"). He was still surrounded by the trappings of wealth. He lived in his own large mansion, had many servants, and drove everywhere in an expensive car. I had no doubt that he could easily have reclaimed everything he'd handed over to others. As nearly as I could tell, all he'd renounced was the civic duty to pay taxes!

For those who would renounce truly, firm truthfulness is a necessity: especially *self*-truthfulness. It is a tendency of human nature to seek constant self-justification. A person will say, "Well, it's true I cheat a little when playing bridge—but I did put twenty dollars in the collection plate last Sunday at church!" Or, "I certainly have my faults, as everyone does, but I'm not guilty of that particular one!" Or, ". . . but I only did that to help him (or her)." Or ". . . that wasn't really wrong of me, because everybody does it."

One might protest, "Yes, I know I smoke a little now and then, but at least I don't drink!" And another might say, "Yes, it's true I take a little sip now and then, but *at least* I don't *smoke!*"

If people are accused of wrong behavior, they usually try to justify it. A car thief will say, "That will teach people not to leave their cars unlocked!" A person who enjoys slandering others will protest, "I'm really only trying to help everyone to be better." Someone who practices fraud will say, "Well, everyone does *something*. It's a dog-eat-dog world, and anyone who doesn't think first for himself will get eaten up."

One day, someone came into my home to do some work, and tracked heavy mud onto the living room carpet. When I protested, he replied, "That's only mud from my boots!"—as if to say, "What do you have against Mother Nature?"

The renunciate should be especially careful not to justify his mistakes. He may, out of moral weakness, succumb to a temptation. If he does so, he should never pretend to himself, or to anyone else, that his indulgence was in some way not wrong. It *was* wrong, simply and completely. Only by utter self-honesty can one hope eventually to come out of delusion.

When Jesus Christ passed through Samaria and met the woman by the well, he recognized her, Yogananda said, as a fallen disciple from past incarnations, and wanted to test her readiness to be re-accepted. He therefore said to her, "Go, call thy husband, and come hither." To that, she answered, "I have no husband." He replied, "Thou hast well said, I have no husband, for thou hast had five husbands; and he whom thou now hast is not thy husband: in that saidst thou truly." (John 4:16–18) Only after she'd spoken the truth did he consent to take her on as a disciple once again.

This is not to say that you should blurt out your defects openly before the world. Be circumspect.

71

Those who are themselves steeped in delusion will attack you like a pack of hungry wolves. Keep your own counsel. Never try, however, to persuade anyone that your wrong desires are anything but delusions.

I faulted those two yogis (whom I mentioned above) for what looked to me like a deficiency of truthfulness. I don't know all the facts, and don't pretend to judge those men. But certainly, *if* they made a promise on which they didn't deliver, they were being untruthful. And it is probably on the basis of that untruth, more even than on those actions, that karmic law will judge them, if in fact it does.

The main purpose of renunciation is to gain the ability to separate truth from error, and thereby to see delusion for what it is: a lie—not pure, certainly, but (once you've seen through it) quite simple!

Be truthful, therefore, even in minor matters. If, for example, you've told someone, "I'll buy a newspaper and read that news," be sure you *obtain* a newspaper at least somehow, and read that article.

If you tell someone, "I'll be there without fail," be very sure you *don't* fail.

Many years ago, in Los Angeles, I went to an Indian friend to borrow a dhoti (an Indian garment for men) for the performance of a play I'd written. A friend of his was there, another Indian. As I was leaving he said, "I will definitely be there." He hadn't asked me where the performance would be. He didn't ask me when. He didn't ask me what it would be about. I knew he wouldn't be there, and of course he wasn't. Why, then, did he tell me he'd "definitely" come?

There is a lamentable tendency in many countries of the East to tell people what a person thinks they want to hear. In Japan, I once asked a salesman if I could buy something for shipment to America. Anxious not to disappoint me, he started affirmatively to nod his head, then stopped and softly muttered, "No."

This tendency is, to my mind, a weakness. In India, some years after Mahatma Gandhi's bold example of truthfulness, I encountered many who tried to follow it by spouting insulting truths. Gandhi never did that! He always showed respect for others' realities. What we should speak is the *helpful, kindly* truth. If a person is stupid, will it help him to tell him so? Of course not! Offer a truth respectfully, and with kindly concern for the person's ability to accept it *usefully.*

With oneself, however, one should be—if not ruthlessly honest, at least impartially so. (Isn't it interesting, how many people consider truthfulness and honesty to be, virtually, synonyms? It's as though they understood that untruthfulness is truly, in some way, dishonest—as though cheating others of what was rightly theirs.)

By strict truthfulness you will align yourself with the Reality behind manifested existence. The completely truthful person develops—so Patanjali declared—the power to bring into manifestation his mere word.

This, by the way, is another reason why you should always tell the truth: Anything you say may—unexpectedly and perhaps undesirably—manifest as reality. Even if your spiritual power is still only slight, you may inadvertently hit a calm moment in the swirl of what Yogananda called "the thwarting crosscurrents of ego," and find your lightest statements become outwardly a reality.

Chapter Eleven

The Sex Issue Revisited

Leaving aside here the survival instinct, which touches on renunciation less directly, let us discuss again how the sincere renunciate ought to deal with this second-most-basic instinct, which, for most people, is paramount in the vice-like grip it has on their consciousness: sex desire. Paramhansa Yogananda called this "the greatest delusion."

What would one do, if he suddenly found an elephant in his bedroom? For many renunciates, that is not far from what it feels like suddenly to have sexual desire raging in their bodies like a tempest.

There are two aspects to the sex instinct. The first is plain animal lust. The second is love—selfless and self-giving. Love, obviously—for one who is seeking liberation—is the better aspect. Love alone is spiritually acceptable. Even in human love, however, there is personal involvement of some kind, which is always limiting to the ego.

The more one allows sex thoughts to enter his mind, the greater will be its hold on ego. Even without sex, however, human love is centered in attachment of some kind. And where there is attachment, there is ego-bondage. This is not, truly speaking, love at all.

I once said to a great woman saint (Ananda Moyi Ma) in India, "All of us [my fellow disciples in America and I] feel great love for you." She replied with appreciation, but impersonally, "There is no love outside of

God's love." And God's love is forever impersonal. This is to say that, although God cares deeply for all of us, individually, He wants nothing from us in return, and can wait for ages, if necessary, for us to return His love selflessly and merge back in Him. Human love is particular; it is for one person, or for a limited number of people. It cannot but be to some extent selfish. Being founded on the emotions, it is circumscribed by personal feelings. And it excludes from its reckoning the needs of mankind in general.

Only divine love is completely impersonal, impartial, self-giving, and concerned for the well-being of others.

Sex affirms the ego, and thereby strengthens it. Its association with love is false. The Spanish expression for human love states it more honestly: "*Yo te quiero—* I *want* you."

This ego-affirmation is another reason why the renunciate path is easier for single persons. To seek the easier way, moreover, is by no means cowardly! One needs every ounce of his own strength to reach the divine goal.

A married person finds it difficult, if not impossible, to feel truly impersonal love for his spouse. Always there lurks the thought, "He (or she) is mine!" Receiving love in return, he/she thinks "I—me—mine!"

"I love you! You love me!" Is that not the theme of innumerable popular songs? Where, in that thought, is the conquest of one's own ego? The more that personal attraction and attachment enter the picture, the more difficult it is to break ego's bonds.

Chapter Twelve

The Stages to Sannyas

Sannyas, or complete renunciation, is not a step to be taken lightly. One must not only be ready for it: he must also convince others of his readiness. To minimize the danger of bias—personal friendship, for example, or predilection—a person should, after successful application to a nayaswami for whom he feels reverence and respect, be approved as a nayaswami by three unrelated persons who are themselves nayaswamis.

First, however, one should go through the stage of *brahmacharya* or *tyaga:* preliminary renunciation. This period should ordinarily last at least six years, so that one becomes quite sure inwardly that he is ready for full sannyas. At this point he should have demonstrated to others also that he truly places God first in his life, and accepts God as his only reality.

How long should a couple wait before they commit themselves to a life of tyaga? I think it should not depend only on age. Young persons, too, may be ready. But all must prove themselves—to others as well as to themselves—before taking this step. The age and time, I think, should vary with the persons concerned.

Men who practice *tyaga* are known as *tyagis;* women, as *tyaginis.* They should do their best to adhere to all the principles in this book. But remember, it is less a matter of specific acts than of the general *direction of one's energy.*

Single men may be called *brahmacharis*; women, similarly, may be called *brahmacharinis*.

Those wishing to become *tyagis* or *brahmacharis* (or their feminine counterparts) must first apply to, and be accepted by, a nayaswami for whom they feel reverence and respect. There is no need for a special ceremony, nor for more than one nayaswami to ordain them. They should, however, repeat the vows listed in Chapter Seventeen that are appropriate for the stage they embrace.

Married people may often do better to wait until they are past the child-rearing years before embracing the stage of tyaga. For one never knows, if children come, what karma they will bring with them. A parent is obligated to respect his child's nature and destiny: his karma, in short. If the child's karma is not consciously to follow the spiritual path—I say "consciously" because all beings, whether they know it or not, are on the path to God—it would do him an injustice to try to force him to embrace a way of life for which he is not ready, and might delay his progress toward God by creating suppression and frustration, and, then, a spirit of rebellion.

Once a couple have passed beyond the likelihood of having children, or have raised their children to the age of (let us say) eighteen, they are free to devote themselves completely, if such be their desire, to the spiritual search. It might be added, moreover, that in cases where a couple cannot have children anyway, or if they are already committed to freedom from sex, they should be allowed to become tyagis. In any case, a tyagi couple should make an extra effort to give their lives wholly to God, to give up sex, and to seek to express God above all in their lives.

They should work hard to rise above anger, desire, and attachment (both to possessions and to one another). They should support one another emotionally, act together cooperatively, and never allow competitiveness to pollute the river of their friendship.

They should seek the guidance of a true guru, or at least of a sincere and wise spiritual teacher. They should strive always to obey him, or at least to follow sincerely the voice of their own higher conscience.

They should learn to look upon every setback in life as a blessing.

☆   ☆   ☆   ☆   ☆

When the time comes that they feel ready to proclaim outwardly their complete commitment to the spiritual path, they may—with permission from their teacher or from others more advanced, whom they respect—embrace formal sannyas and become *swamis*. Because they ought, at this stage, to have reached the point where they no longer see themselves as men or women, renunciates of both sexes should be given the same title: *swami*. It is no longer fitting for women renunciates to receive the feminine version of this title, *swamini*.

Because this is a new renunciate order, I recommend that all swamis in it receive, in addition to the title, the designation *naya*—that is to say, "new." Thus, my own name would be *Nayaswami* Kriyananda.

Names may include the customary "ananda," meaning (as I've said already) "bliss." They may also, however, simply indicate some spiritual quality, thus: *Nayaswami Seva* (meaning, service). There will be no indication in the name as to whether the person is male or female. As to the choice of name, this can be left to the discretion of the individual, and of those who initiate him or her.

Regardless of any future slip in one's dedication to one's ideals, so long as the *direction* of his aspiration is upward, there should be no outward punishment or "demotion" from whatever status he has attained.

Because many of the virtues mentioned here are questions of attitude—and even sexual self-control is too personal to be ascertained objectively—one's worthiness to continue to keep the title *tyagi* or *nayaswami* must be left up to the individual's conscience. There comes a point where only God is qualified to judge.

I have tried to make it clear, and want to emphasize again, that this new renunciate order is not limited to the members of Ananda, which is the community I myself founded in 1969. The order should, however, be given a clear form, and cannot be encouraged to flourish unchecked like the growth of mushrooms in the forest.

This order has no clear link to the Ananda system of *sadhakas*, *sevakas*, and life members. It is intended to stand alone. Nor is it by any means inevitable that people will become nayaswamis simply by virtue of their being leaders at Ananda. I think the new order must flower from those people who are swamis already.

New systems inevitably meet opposition. I can imagine people scoffing at our nayaswamis as *mayaswamis*! Let it be. A certain amount of ridicule is good for the soul, and for the freedom-seeking ego!

Chapter Thirteen

The Habit

One's habit, in Western monastic terminology, signifies the garb of a monk or nun. A habit is a protection and a constant self-reminder of the way of life one has embraced. Paramhansa Yogananda, during his lifetime, was somewhat averse to the wearing of a monastic garb by his disciples. His message was for the world. He didn't want to convey the message, therefore, that what he taught was only for the few. He did say, however, that it would become suitable in the future for his monastic disciples to indicate the special dedication of their spiritual calling by wearing suitable clothing.

I think it is time, now that his message has become widely known in the world, for monks and nuns—though perhaps cautiously at first—to wear that suitable habit.

Brahmacharis and brahmacharinis should dress in a golden yellow. I suggest that tyagis and tyaginis wear white. Since, however, those working in the world may find any habit inconvenient, I will leave to them the question of when, where, how, etc. Let them decide individually, or as a group.

Nayaswamis, as I said earlier, should wear a bright royal blue.

A simple habit has been designed, the same style for men as for women: *pyjamas* (the uncreased cotton slacks worn in India), and a long tunic top, similar to the Indian *kurta* , but without buttons, closing with a zipper in the back.As to when this garb should be worn, I would say that it depends on general custom and acceptability. Changes occur more naturally when they are introduced gradually. Ideally, however, the monastic garb should be worn wherever convenient, as a sign of a person's sincere commitment, and as a personal protection from worldly influences.

More on this important subject, however, in the next chapter.

Chapter Fourteen

The Widespread Need for Renunciation

This is certainly not an age (if any such ever existed) when one's spiritual aspiration ought to be hidden from others. The influence of worldly delusion is widespread and powerful. Our day seems, indeed, an example of those times described by Lord Krishna in the Bhagavad Gita: "O Bharata (Arjuna)! whenever virtue (dharma) declines, and vice (adharma) is in the ascendant, I incarnate Myself on earth (as an avatar). Appearing from age to age in visible form, I come to destroy evil and to re-establish virtue." (4:7,8)

One's devotion to God is a very private feeling, and ought never to be displayed publicly lest it become hypocrisy. If, however, one conceals from others his *dedication* to truth, he may (as I suggested at the end of the last chapter) deprive himself of a useful protection. He may also merit the accusation of being, spiritually, a coward.

This is an age when people need to "stand up and be counted." It isn't enough for them to remain merely a statistic: "Such and such a percentage of people believe in God," and so on. It is a time for active participation in the outer struggle: light against darkness.

What is needed today is a spiritual army of souls demonstrating—not militantly or aggressively, but with sincerity declared—their commitment to higher values, to God, and (in this age of hyper-advertising) to a firm rejection of worldly values.

Just consider a modern street in the pulsing heart of any city, with crowds milling about, and rushing here and there bent on the business of profit, acquisition, and involvement with desires. In any such crowd there may be a few people whose thoughts are focused on higher goals, but who, on beholding that crowd, would gain any inkling of the fact?

Go to any exhibition of modern art. Most of what you see there will be atrocious. How—one wonders—did the craze ever begin for such distortions of good taste? I imagine a few people standing before a painting, utterly baffled, but looking cautiously right and left to see if anyone in the group can make *anything* of what they are beholding. Most people are not sure of their own taste, and are therefore unwilling to commit themselves to either a positive or a negative judgment. No one wants to be thought naive, or completely lacking in artistic sense. So then, finally, someone may dare to say, "I do like it!" Others around him, hearing his remark, may dare then to repeat, "So do I!" though only with a confidence born of imitation. The doubters in the crowd may decide, finally, that safety lies in numbers. Hesitantly, but with increasing courage, they join the chorus. "We all *love* it!" And such, finally, becomes the verdict. *Vox populi, vox Dei!*

I saw a movie years ago in which a young, aspiring singer made it to the stage at last, before a large audience. She sang beautifully—after all, that's why she was chosen for the part!—but the director felt it wasn't enough to leave it to the movie audience to be convinced by this simple demonstration. Repeated shots of individuals in the play-audience were necessary, showing, by stages, first an individual here and there, then groups of people, and finally the whole crowd smiling, nodding to one another, and in the end standing and clapping wild approval. Thus, those who saw the movie concluded without a single doubt that the performer had, indeed, sung well.

Such is human nature. Those who are blessed with the discrimination to be able to judge a truth on its own merits are very few.

Thus, if you have reached the point in your spiritual evolution where you realize that the true goal of life is to find God, you may also decide, dispassionately, that this realization will come eventually to everyone, each in his own time. You may, therefore, decide to seek liberation only for yourself. Such becomes, indeed, the final decision arrived at by most souls. After countless incarnations of suffering the limitations, deprivations, and disappointments of *maya*, they feel it is enough, now, to merge back into Infinite Bliss, and to view the whole scene of manifested existence as a "blessed riddance."

If God, however, takes the trouble from time to time to send an avatar-savior into the world to "destroy evil and to re-establish virtue," one cannot but feel He will be pleased if at least a few of those who are still seeking liberation help Him in this mighty undertaking.

I read a book years ago about someone who regressed people in time to a point before their present incarnation on earth. He asked each of them, "Why did you choose to reincarnate at this particular time?" All of them said they knew it would be a time of great stress and hardship. None of them, however, spoke of the sufferings they would endure. All spoke, instead, of the great opportunity this life would give them for soul advancement.

Today is not, in other words, a time for "dropping out."

84

A new order of renunciation would lose much of its spiritual merit were it kept a secret from all but the chosen few. It is desperately important today for people who long for a higher way of life to be reassured that they are not alone. If there is safety in numbers, there is also the need for reassurance from a sufficiency of numbers.

I myself, when I finally (at the age of twenty-one) realized that the only possible way of life for me was to seek God, began to wonder if possibly I was losing my mind. I had never read about saints who had sought Him, to say nothing of anyone who had actually found Him. Might I, I asked myself seriously, be going crazy? I sought every alternative I could imagine to this search. Among other things, I tried to live a simple life in the country, among simple country folk. The experiment proved a disaster. The "simple country people" I met did nothing at all for me in terms of helping me even to find peace of mind. It wasn't until I came upon *Autobiography of a Yogi*, by Paramhansa Yogananda, that I found the support I needed in my almost-desperate yearning for God.

And then I found that there were many others, in fact, in America who shared my ideals. I had found the path quite on my own. What a help it would have been, had I even known there was a path to be found!

The age we live in has seen much violence, fear, suffering, destruction, and spiritual turmoil; it is destined to see a great deal more. We are entering a time of widespread economic depression. A prophecy I read in India described this as being a time "when there will be weeping in every home." People are confused, uncertain, and unhappy. They look to one another for guidance, but, everywhere they look, they find only ignorance. Like the proverbial ostrich, they try to hide from uncertainty by burying their heads in the sand of unending distractions.

It is time, certainly, for those few to band together who know *from within* that there is a higher way of life. At least they can demonstrate clearly, in some outward manner, that they—so few in all that crowd!—have a more valid goal than mere absorption in materialism and ego-consciousness.

A renunciate order in which people demonstrate their commitment not by shouting their beliefs, waving flags and banners, or in other ways campaigning outwardly, but simply by the garb they wear—this, surely, would be a minimal way to "stand up and be counted."

I would like now, therefore, to plead with my readers: If your heart resonates with what I have written so far, then look for some way to commit yourself to it formally, and to make your commitment known to others.

I don't say, Join Ananda. Rather I say, Wherever you are, and whatever your path or stage of life, join this order; embrace its ideals; commit yourself to them *in action*. Don't shrug helplessly and say, "What beautiful concepts. I hope enough people do something about them." *Become*, yourself, one of those people! If you are married, discuss this way of life with your spouse. I haven't asked you to roam the highways like the sannyasis of old. I've asked you simply to change your own attitude toward life. Some couples would admittedly find it difficult—in the streets, or even about the home—to wear the garb of tyaga, but on special spiritual occasions, surely, they can do so without fearing lest the finger of outrage be pointed at them.

Brahmacharis, brahmacharinis, and swamis (whether married or unmarried) should be less reticent. To show the courage of their convictions seems to me right, and even necessary.

Should they dress that way in the privacy of their homes? That, I think, should be left to personal choice. But the face they show to the world should normally include not only their eyes, mouths, and noses, but also their life commitment. There are times, granted, when one wants to remain incognito. To have to suffer challenges and questions, moreover, every time one walks abroad or gets onto a plane does seem a quite unnecessary penance. As I said in the last chapter, such a social change must be introduced gradually.

Paramhansa Yogananda wanted our daily garb to be normal. He himself, when in America, dressed in a normal business suit. He demonstrated the different-ness of his calling, however, by wearing a scarf—not orange, in fact, but white—covering his chest. In India, he wore the traditional orange garb of an Indian swami. His style of dress was not particularly impor-tant to him. As he put it, it is the *heart*, not the body, that should wear the luster of devotion.

Yet he did say that he wanted us someday to wear monastic garbs. Has that day arrived yet? Perhaps not in the West. In India? More probably. He himself wore his swami robe everywhere during his first days in America. Just when it was that he changed this prac-tice I don't know, but I imagine it was when he found that people were more distracted by it, in everyday life, than inspired.

What he did have us do was wear monastic garb at special public functions, and as ministers in the churches. He also told his present successor (Daya Mata) that monastic garbs would someday be more generally appropriate for us. From these guidelines, I draw the following conclusions:

First, that he does want us, now, to wear them in suitable settings, but to be sensitive also to what *is* suitable, and what is not.

Second, that although suitable settings would certainly include formal spiritual events, they need not include the settings of everyday life.

Third, that gradually, as we ourselves feel comfortable wearing them in our own setting, it would become suitable for us to wear them always.

Fourth, that when we are in public, it would be only right to wear them, once public acceptance of them has become widespread.

Fifth, that when we are traveling (for instance, by train or by plane), it would be better for the present *not* to wear them.

Sixth, that in India it might be suitable to wear them much sooner than in the West—maybe even now.

Some couples would find it very awkward to wear a special garb except at public functions. They can, however—indeed, *all* monastics can—wear something suggestive of their spiritual vocation: golden yellow for brahmacharis; white for tyagis; blue for nayaswamis. They could wear shirts or blouses of the appropriate color. When men wear suits, they could wear an appropriately colored handkerchief folded visibly in the breast pocket; women could do the same with scarves, sashes, or something else that is suitable. Perhaps shirts or blouses could be designed not to have buttons in the front, and to be slipped on over the head.

Short sleeves in hot weather? Well, why not?

An appropriate pin, worn somewhere on the chest, or perhaps on a pendant, would also be a means of declaring one's renunciate identity.

The point in any case is not to stand up and be counted *by others*, but as a signal to those who share your ideals: "You are not alone." At first, this might not protect the monastic from worldly intrusions, but gradually the signal would become more and more widely known and accepted. The time when it becomes widely respected will be, I suggest, when a monastic might feel free to go anywhere, fully dressed in the suitable garb.

Chapter Fifteen

A Need for Proper Education

A brahmachari is one who practices *brahmacharya*—a word that has become associated mainly, over time, with sexual self-control, though its full and true meaning is "flowing with Brahma." To flow with God, or divine inspiration, is to be in tune with the Lord in every aspect of one's life.

Brahmacharya is also the first of the four classically designated *ashrams*, or stages of life: the student stage. The other three ashrams are *grihastha* (householder), *vanaprastha* (partially retired from worldly life), and *sannyas* (full renunciation).

There is therefore a special link between the first and the fourth stages of life. Both of them were specifically directed toward offering one's life up to God: the first stage, in preparation for seeing Him as life's true goal; the fourth, in devoting one's life to the quest for liberation. The ashram system in India was specifically directed toward living in godly ways. It originated during a higher age, when the concept of life's purpose was understood widely enough to become crystallized in an actual system. Though such is not nowadays the case, there is at least the possibility of creating examples within society where it can be practiced: in special schools, for example, where children can be educated in this system; and in separate communities, which members join with the conscious intention of living spiritually.

I should add that such communities already exist. I myself have founded eight of them. In most of them, moreover, we already have "Living Wisdom" schools based on the principles expounded in my book, *Education for Life.*

Even our Living Wisdom schools, however, still need to introduce the concept of renunciation. Thus, although in a sense we teach the children to "flow with Brahma," we have yet to introduce more fully the concept of renunciation, whether as tyagis, brahmacharis, or as swamis.

I suggest that it is time now to give serious thought to teaching the need for self-control *before* the growing adolescent finds himself trapped in habits that must, in time, ruin his life, or may at least make it very difficult to steer it in an upward direction.

Already in our Ananda schools we teach the need, and give reasons, for upholding higher values in life than the usual craze for money, fame, and worldly power. Even when a child desires these goals, he is taught to see them as a means for doing good in the world. Ananda children learn the benefits, *to themselves*, of including other people's happiness in their own. They are taught the importance of self-control. And they learn, in addition, the value to themselves of all true virtues.

In national tests, our children usually score in the ninety-fifth percentile.

When they graduate or go to other schools, they invariably become outstanding students in their new situations, and often rise to become leaders, whether of the student body, or in the world.

Children at Ananda schools learn not to tamper with hallucinogenic drugs or with alcohol. They learn self-discipline, concentration, cooperation with others, and the importance of living by high spiritual ideals.

We have not yet been able strongly enough to emphasize sexual self-control. The importance of deep spiritual commitment is, I think, not so much taught as implied. I suggest that, in future, not only Ananda schools but schools everywhere include all these ideals in their curriculum. For as the children are raised, so does a society become.

I suggest that, in time, *gurukuls** be created as in ancient India. It would be well, even today, for people to study that system and see which of its features might be adopted.

One thing I recommend is that boys and girls be separated during their adolescent years. Sexual awakening is a time of great emotional upheaval. A child needs to learn how to cope with new feelings that, with puberty, are virtually inflicted on him by Nature itself. Separation of the sexes can give the adolescent a chance to learn for himself how to handle the sudden, disruptive imperatives of his own body.

In my book, *Education for Life,* I state that each of the six-year periods of life leading to adulthood has its own specific needs. During the first six years, the primary need is to develop physical coordination. During the next six years, until the age of twelve, there is a need to channel one's emotions rightly; from twelve to eighteen, the need comes to direct the will with discrimination; and from eighteen to twenty-four, the need is to hone and refine the intellect. Ideally, education should (and, in the actual school of life, does) continue to the age of twenty-four, after which time one has—as well as he ever will have—the tools to cope with objective reality.

The "will" years, from twelve to eighteen, are ex-

* Schools—generally, outdoors—in ancient India, where the teaching was on all areas of life, including spiritual practice, and was done by gurus or sages.

tremely important for inculcating in the growing child an understanding of how to use his will power for *self-*conquest, not for the conquest of others: how to rule himself, and not to impose his will on others.

An adolescent's energy is often directed *primarily* toward making a conquest of someone of the other sex. A boy thinks, "How can I win her affection?" A girl thinks, "How can I best attract him?" It is important for both to learn not only the "facts of life," but how to direct that knowledge upward, toward a higher understanding of the uses and abuses of the sex instinct. Sound reasons need to be given, to which the adolescent can relate intelligently.

Every generation considers itself the first ever to discover sex. Adolescence is a time of exaggerated ego-consciousness, arising from a heightened spirit of competition, which develops with puberty and the following "will" years. Teenagers may tend to be over-confident—almost ridiculously so—or just the opposite: to develop an almost pathetic sense of utter incompetence, and an ego-paralyzing inferiority complex.

I suggest even what, in some societies, has been called a "rite of passage." This rite should be conducted for children of both sexes, and not only—as has been traditionally the case—for boys. Boys, especially, should be taught that what is at first pleasurable often ends in misery, if the energy is not brought under control and wisely directed. Girls should be taught that, while it is easy to attract boys with "feminine wiles," they will lose the boys' respect and will only, in the end, alienate them. Each should be taught above all to *respect* the other, and should be given good reasons not to view anyone in terms of conquest.

I suggest the rite be conducted by several adult (that is to say, truly mature) men or women—men, obviously, for the boys, and women for the girls. It could be a formal ceremony, at which every participating adult addresses some specific aspect of the meaning of true maturity.

There could then be a fire ceremony, into which the participating children symbolically cast their former expectations: that of being forever cared for and supported (emotionally and financially), and that of being childishly dependent on the will of others (of their parents, of course, especially). From now on, they'll need to act, will, and think more for themselves. Teenagers have a natural tendency, anyway, to test the knife-edge of their will. It seems wise to help them to direct this tendency toward their own highest good.

Each child may then be given a token of his acceptance into this new phase of life: perhaps a yellow badge of some kind, which can be pinned on clothing as a constant reminder, especially to oneself, of the high principles that have been embraced.

The ceremony should consist of a prayer and a pledge. The prayer should be for divine guidance in one's life, for God's acceptance of one's devotion, and for the grace to be able always to share with others whatever blessings one receives in life.

The fire ceremony should be accompanied by the *Mahamrityunjaya* mantra:

> *Aum, triambakam yajaamahe sugandim, pushti-vaardhanam*
> *Urvaarukameva bhandhanaan mrityor mokshiya Maamritaat.*
>
> (We worship the three-eyed One who is fragrant and who nourishes all beings.
> (May He liberate us from death and bring us immortality, even as the cucumber is severed from its bondage to the creeper.)

94

After repeating it three times, as a demand for liberation from all physical, mental, and spiritual karmas, the participants should cast a handful of rice into the fire to symbolize the burning of the seeds of their past karma.

The pledge, after an invocation to God and His great saints, may be as follows:

"I know that that action is best which most truly brings me happiness.

"I understand that I am happiest when I include the happiness of others in my own.

"I will seek always to be useful and helpful to others, to society, and to all mankind, and will try to find happiness not only for myself, but for everyone.

"I will always be grateful to my parents for the good they have given me, and will forgive them for any hurts, for I know that I myself will suffer most if I hold negative feelings in my heart toward anyone.

"I will treat my body as a temple of God, and will do my best to keep it clean and holy: as a place where I can humbly worship.

"I will try to live always by the highest ideals—for my own and for others' happiness and well-being."

After each verse in the above pledge, each participant should offer a small teaspoon of ghee (clarified butter) into the flames as a symbol of the purity of his intentions.

Chapter Sixteen

A Vision of the Future

Now that we are over one hundred years into the ascending Dwapara Yuga of energy, will our future be smoother and brighter? I'd like to think so. Realistically, however, and unfortunately, the signs point to an immediate future, at least, that seems neither smooth nor bright.

The constricting attitudes of Kali Yuga—dogmatic resistance, and even opposition, to new ideas; narrow loyalties; religious persecution; fixed beliefs rather than openness to the demonstrations of experience; authority based on social or institutional position rather than on personal merit; hierarchical, rather than democratic, power; ignorance of, and resistance to, any point of view but one's own; brute force as the surest way of settling differences of opinion—all these are still present, and militate against the more fluid rays of Dwapara. As nature, according to science, never makes sudden leaps, so also human consciousness moves only gradually to new levels of understanding.

There comes a time, however, as the stresses between two opposing points of view build up, when something snaps. Over the past century, and—more generally—over the past three hundred years, there has also been slowly building up an openness to new possibilities; a broadening of loyalties to include awareness of the rights of people elsewhere in the world, of other nations, races, and those with other interests; a growing outcry against religious fanaticism; an awareness that belief alone cannot guarantee any truth; a growing awareness that true merit is individual, and depends not on rank, social position, or popular acclaim; and a greater dependence on negotiation instead of brute force.

How do things now stand, in the present year, Dwapara 309? We see tension building between monetary greed (avarice) and a Dwapara understanding of increasing respect for the needs of all. A time seems to be approaching for an explosion of some kind; perhaps, first, in the form of a massive, widespread depression.

People sought a bloated supply of money. Very well, they will get it—in the form of a depression that will give them so much money, through hyper-inflation, that money will no longer be worth the paper it is printed on. The resultant misery—since people wouldn't learn otherwise—will end in a completely new financial system.

People thought mere systems would guarantee them the peace and prosperity they'd always wanted. Very well, Karl Marx was therefore given the inspiration, drawn to him by world karma, to provide humanity with the quintessence of every evil of Kali Yuga, in the form of communism. This model of twisted idealism promises equality to all men, and brotherly love on earth, but instead it has given repression, fear, almost universal spying, a security based on universal control, and the power of a few to suppress everyone in the name of lockstep togetherness. The supreme power is the state, which of course means the few ruthless individuals who run the state and can bully everyone else. The economic fallacies of communism aren't really the primary issue. The true issue, rather, is individual freedom of conscience as opposed to mental slavery.

Depression will bring many other evils. Paramhansa Yogananda once, in my hearing, after expressing exasperation with "city hall" and its endless regulations, made the frequently heard, but lightly intended, comment, "There ought to be a revolution!" The Master paused a moment, then said more quietly, "There *will* be one."

What about global war? When a nation has less than other nations, it not infrequently seeks the "solution" of invading countries that are better off. There are, moreover, intensely conflicting ideologies: communism versus all other systems; Islam versus all other religions. We have already seen Germany seeking "Lebensraum" (living space), and justifying its actions by the pseudo-Darwinian slogan, "survival of the fittest." Need we look further for more causes of future conflict?

If even one atom bomb is dropped, there will almost certainly be retribution. Soon, atom bombs will be dropping everywhere. Sri D.R. Kaarthikeyan, who once held the same post as J. Edgar Hoover (head of the FBI in America) in a country (India) much more populous than America, told me that there are over thirty thousand *known* atomic weapons stockpiled in the world. One cannot but wonder: How many *unknown* weapons of that kind are stored also?

The comforting thought is that any atomic war will be blessedly brief: it cannot be a long-drawn-out affair. The *un*comforting thought is that it will be brief because there won't be enough people left to continue fighting!

I suspect that quite a few billion people will die in such a holocaust, and many more people later on, owing to radioactive pollution. How many, of the more than six billion people on our planet, will be left to carry forward the banner of civilization? My guess is, maybe one billion, or maybe a few hundred million. Perhaps even fewer. My Guru once predicted, "Europe will be devastated. Russia will be annihilated!" Civilization itself will undergo a complete overhaul.

When I visited Cambodia in 1958, I was aware of what felt to me like a dark cloud over that country. We know the tragedy Cambodia later suffered. More recently, I have felt a similar cloud over Germany, though it seems to me less dark. Who knows?

Cities have become one of the great curses of mankind. They nurture crime, avarice, cutthroat competition, and indifference to one's neighbor. In the past, people gravitated to cities because that was where the jobs were. Now, however, especially with the invention of home computers, people are finding that they can conduct even such business as buying and selling from their homes in the country. There will, I believe, be a massive exodus to the country. Cities will be destroyed, either from within by that mass exodus, or from without by atomic weapons. Perhaps cities of the future will contain the much-more-reasonable figure of twenty or thirty thousand residents.

Who will emerge victorious—if anyone can be called victor amid such devastation? Yogananda said America's karma is such that no one will be able to defeat her.

People always like to point the finger of blame, especially against those who are more successful than themselves. Yogananda said that America has some bad karma also—for its treatment of the American Indians; for dropping the first atom bomb. On the other hand, there has been no other nation in history that, after being attacked, has gone on to beat its enemy, and then stooped to help the attacking country to regain its former prosperity. Cynics have sneered, "Yes, but America, too, gained by this 'generosity.'" True. This is a description of enlightened selfishness, so why fault it?

My Guru didn't mention the treatment, in the southern states, of black slaves from Africa. The fact that he didn't do so, at least at that time, leads me to wonder whether he didn't see that human atrocity in a positive light also. For it has provided a segment of the black population with the sophistication to lift their brothers and sisters elsewhere out of the karma that led their continent to be called "the dark continent."

The races of man are not validly defined by such superficial differences as skin coloring. Yogananda said that the true races are defined by the basic differences in human temperament—that is to say, by human nature's progressive levels of refinement, anciently described by the caste system. Those differences are not hereditary, but indicate rather the stages individuals have reached in the evolution of their spiritual consciousness. Yogananda once said, "I don't see why people talk about whites and blacks. Under the skin, they are all red!"

During the descending cycle of yugas, I think Africa as a whole, including Egypt, must have fallen spiritually, through the widespread practice of black magic. Even today, this practice exists everywhere on that continent. A black friend of mine, an American, visited Nigeria several years ago and commented later, "It showed me the positive aspect of slavery!" For blacks in America will, I also feel, become a liberating force for blacks everywhere—not politically, but spiritually.

They will inspire a very great upliftment among black people throughout the world.

However, I think that the "dark continent" may also need the purifying fires of a great destruction. I once read a book in which the author, a psychiatrist, instead of regressing his patients to former lives, tried to take them forward into the future. Whether or not his findings were valid it is impossible to say, but I was struck by the statements of some people that Africa and the Near East will become uninhabitable for a long time as a result of atomic radiation.

Paramhansa predicted, "Someday, America and India will join hands and lead the world on a peaceful path of balanced spiritual and material efficiency." Swami Rama Tirtha, a saint from India who came to America early in the twentieth century, predicted also, "Someday you Americans will take our Indian teachings, make them practical, and bring them back to my people."

Depression, world war, widespread devastation: these seem sufficient causes for alarm. However, there is a likelihood of even greater trouble on our horizon!

Heretofore, man has been accustomed to think of this planet as complete in itself, unaffected by outside influences. Our knowledge of the physical universe is still very young indeed. In my own lifetime even, when I was a schoolboy in England during the late 1930s, one of the teachers said to me, "Do you realize that all the stars we see at night belong to only one star system? It was recently discovered that the so-called nebula in Andromeda is another entire star system. So far, one—and perhaps even *two*—other such systems have been found!" Those systems were dubbed, "island universes." Since then they've been named galaxies, and astronomers claim that there are over a hundred billion of them in the universe.

This vast universe is not the mere mechanism that present-day astronomers think it. It might be called, rather, a great, living organism. Indeed, it is not only alive: it is *conscious*. And when there is either harmony or disharmony in the consciousness of a large number of beings on one planet, they attract to it commensurate blessings or punishment.

Padre Pio, a great saint of the last century in Italy, predicted there would descend on our earth, in the future, three days of darkness. He warned people to stay indoors at that time, for the atmosphere would be, at that time, dangerously polluted.

Someone told me he had read of a similar prediction made by Paramhansa Yogananda in one of his writings. I have not read those words myself, but I was present in church one Sunday when he spoke of the coming depression. He interrupted that discussion for a moment to cry loudly, "You don't know what a *terrible cataclysm* is coming!"

What could be the cause of such an event? It couldn't be due to a severe volcanic eruption, for the effect of any such occurrence would last for years, not merely for three days.

Could it be some heavenly body striking the earth with such violence that the earth's spinning would be temporarily stopped—until a natural inner impetus sets it spinning again? If so, the other side of the earth will suffer an equally punishing three days of sunlight. But in this case, one wonders how to account for that polluted atmosphere. I confess it is beyond my comprehension, but I am convinced *something* terrible will happen. I have also read theories that the predicted impact would be caused by a large body striking the moon when it is new, thus throwing a cloud of dust that would cease to come between us and the sun only as the moon in its orbit moved out of the sun's way.

Yogananda (and also Padre Pio) said that those who love God will be protected. I don't suppose, however, that protection means that none of them will die. In a hundred years, nearly everyone on this planet will be gone from here anyway. This world might be described (though ignorantly) as a giant concentration camp, in which only a few die peacefully in their beds. The horror is dissipated by the fact that people "check out" one by one. Die they must, however, and many of them go painfully. The freedom from pain comes after death. God's protection, then, must be understood to mean that, for those who love Him, death will be very easy.

Death itself, indeed, *is* easy, and very pleasant because of its accompanying freedom from confinement within these heavy walls of flesh. Suffering, to the extent that it accompanies death, is only mental: the pain of broken attachments. The very longing, however, for earthly enjoyments prevents people from enjoying heaven itself for very long. In time, they will have to take birth again in a physical body, and will keep on reincarnating here, or on some other planet, until their last desire has been fulfilled or dissipated.

Paramhansa Yogananda once—I was not present on that occasion—told a group of monks, "Someday you all will have to build again from scratch." Did this mean that the buildings on his properties, and especially on Mt. Washington (his headquarters), would be demolished—perhaps by an atom bomb? I think it all too possible. But would this constitute divine protection? It might, if his organization has strayed too far from his true intentions for it. I remember him saying on one occasion, very forcefully, "If ever I see . . . [here I deliberately omit a few words, but it concerned something within the organization], then, no matter where I am in space, I shall return and *destroy* this organization!"

The sufferings to come will be the result, finally, of mankind's having turned away from God. Therefore I state urgently that our new renunciate order is very desperately needed by mankind, and that it should not be confined to only one organization. Many thousands of people need, now, to "stand up and be counted."

Will the earth be destroyed? Yogananda said, "Definitely not." He once said, "I prophesy you will see a new world! a world of peace, harmony, and prosperity. The earth will know no wars for hundreds of years, so tired will they be of violence of all kinds."

The earth, in this new Dwapara age, will see inconceivable progress, not only with great advancement—scientific and otherwise—on all levels of life, but there will even be travel to distant planets. Dwapara Yuga is a time when man will penetrate the illusion of space. If space is indeed an illusion, then the most distant galaxy must be no farther away, really, than our own feet! Perhaps man will then be able even to travel to galaxies that now seem impossibly distant from us. As regards space travel *to* our earth, Master said, after the flurry of sightings of UFOs in 1949, "They are indeed visitors from other planets." In fact, he said, the universe is teeming with life. A fellow disciple once told me that our Guru had said there is even life on the sun, where entities live in bodies of gas.

The concept of small, intentional communities (like Ananda) will, Yogananda said, "spread like wildfire," and will become an important pattern of life in the future.

If someone living today were to go back in time and speak about the wonders of the present age, he might be sent to a madhouse. Toward the end of the nineteenth century, I have heard it said, the head of the Patent Office proposed in all seriousness that the Patent Office be closed "because everything that could possibly be invented has been invented already." I've read that this report is apocryphal, but it fits the case perfectly—like an Italian saying, "*Se non è vero, è ben trovato*," which is to say, "If it isn't true, it's well perceived anyway."

Virtually everything we associate with modern life has been discovered, invented, or put to widespread use since the beginning of the twentieth century: radio, telephone, television, microwave ovens, cars, airplanes, jet airplanes, rocket travel—well, the list goes on and on.

I myself grew up in Romania, which at that time was an almost medieval country. When a plane flew overhead, we would all go outdoors and wave to it. One year, in an effort at modernization, the whole country went, by mistake, on daylight *losing* time! Romanians themselves were quite casual about such modern conveniences as train travel. A friend of mine told me that she had once traveled by second class in Romania. When the conductor came by, he asked her in astonishment, "What are you doing in this class?" "Why, can't you see? I have a second class ticket." The conductor responded with a humorous smile, "Oh, that doesn't matter *in Romania*! Get on up in the first class with everyone else!"

For me personally, then, the change to the twentieth century has been particularly striking. But these changes are minimal compared to what will come over the next two thousand years.

Chapter Seventeen

The Vows of Renunciation

Any pledge one takes—what to speak of any vow—should have the force behind it of personal conviction.

A mere pledge states, "I am not yet certain, for I don't fully know myself in these matters. But this is the direction I would like to take."

A vow should have more force behind it than a pledge. The vow of brahmacharya or tyaga must be backed by sufficient conviction to be able to say, "I am sure, now, that this is the direction I want to go, and I will build my life around it." This vow, in other words, implies more than the mere statement, "I will try." One has walked the length of the counter, and has made his decision.

We must always accept the truth, however, that the growth to perfection is directional: it is not a sudden leap from the valley floor to the mountaintop. Only those can make such a leap who are already highly advanced, and who don't really need any vows at all, for they have attained the very purpose of those vows.

There is always the temptation, on the upward climb, to turn back in discouragement and declare, "Oh, but I find that it really *is*, after all, too high for me!" There is a possibility of discouragement, of intense fatigue, and even of such thoughts as, "I wonder if I locked the back door of my house; maybe I'd better go back and make sure everything is still safe"—a reawakened desire, in other words, to return to the lowlands of maya.

A vow is important. Verbalizing a commitment gives it extra force. The spoken word directs power, and reinforces one's determination to be true.

When one starts up a mountainside, however, no matter how strong his initial will to climb it, he can't know everything that awaits him farther on; he can only deal with the present, and with his expectations of the journey. As the way grows steeper, he may have to check his heart, his breathing, his muscular endurance, to see whether he is in fact up to the whole climb. The more obstacles he overcomes, of course, the greater the confidence he gains.

First, however, he must pledge himself to make a valiant attempt. It is useless to make firm promises until one has reached a level of such inner certainty that, for him, the only alternative to the climb is death itself.

It doesn't matter to him, then, that he isn't fully aware of what lies ahead. What if he finds he must scale a steep cliff? What if he falls, and goes crashing onto the rocks below? His courage must be such that he will press forward no matter what the difficulties. The true renunciate is one who is willing to face *any* obstacle in his struggle to reach the goal, for he knows that there is no acceptable alternative. Even if he slips, his *intention* never falters. And even if he is killed, he knows that he belongs utterly and completely to God alone. He is fully determined to reach God, no matter how many lifetimes it takes, and never to accept a lesser ideal. He vows never to stop until he reaches the top.

The vow of brahmacharya, and also that of tyaga, are vows truly, and not mere resolutions. One who takes these vows must abide by them "come hell or high water!" as the saying goes. These vows, then, are not for weaklings. And penalties exist for breaking them.

What penalties? They are primarily inward, in one's own consciousness. There is the possibility, also—though it is a trivial one—that one who breaks his vows may find himself ostracized by people who share the same high principles, but who would never, themselves, dare to embrace them fully. Disappointment in oneself is what can be really devastating. One's will may become paralyzed for a long time—preventing him, perhaps, from ever again accepting another challenge with confidence.

When a person becomes disappointed in himself, that letdown may take the form of only a temporary weakness, followed in time by renewed determination. If, however, it amounts to a deep acceptance of failure or defeat, it may last his whole life. These consequences are up to him.

I knew someone who turned back for a time to the world, and then, with great will power, resumed her spiritual search. Her monastic associates challenged her, "How can you dare to show your face here again?"

She shot back the reply: "Do you expect me to worship my mistakes?!"

It must be understood, however, that none of us lives alone in space, with no one and nothing to influence him. When you turn toward God, the Lord Himself, and His angels, come to your assistance. Everything worthwhile that you accomplish from then on will, to a great extent, be due to that grace, and not to your efforts alone. If you turn away from that grace, however, you may find yourself abandoned by it. Grace will only reach out to save you if you have already proved yourself deeply sincere in your commitment. If you have yet to earn that extraordinary grace, and if the divine forces are not convinced that you really want God alone, they may decide to let you learn life's lessons more thoroughly as you wander again, for a time, on your own. As Yogananda put it, "God says, I will wait."

By abandoning your vow, you may actually open yourself to contrary, satanic influences. The greater your rejection of the good, the more powerful those negative influences will be in your life.

Yogananda also said reassuringly, however, "God is no tyrant." If you really do want Him above all else, He will take you back into His all-loving, all-embracing arms. It will depend above all on when you, yourself, are ready. He, as I said, is always there, waiting for you. It depends, you see, on the strength of your own will.

There is no need, certainly, for the imposition of social strictures on any failed renunciate. Unless his failure is accompanied by self-justifying condemnation of "God and all that crazy crowd," he deserves people's compassion. The inner penalties he draws will be what he deserves. Who is man, that he should presume to say what the dictates of karmic law shall be?

I submit now the vows for brahmacharis, tyagis, pilgrims, and nayaswamis respectively. Each set of vows will be given its own separate page.

Renunciate Vow of Brahmacharya

I understand, and fully accept, that the true purpose of life for all human beings is to seek God.

In pursuit of that goal, I offer my own life unreservedly to seeking my Divine Source.

I will retain no ego-gratifying goal in my life, but will strive always, and above all, to please God.

I will look upon life as God's dream-drama, and also dream-entertainment. I will accept as His gift whatever comes to me in life.

I renounce attachment to things, people, places, and all self-definitions—except one: I will define myself always as a child of God, and will obey whatever guidance He gives me.

I offer to Thee, Lord, my life, my desires, my attachments, and the fruit of all my labors.

Bless me, and strengthen me, that I become ever more perfect in this, my holy vow.

Renunciate Vow of Tyaga

I understand, and fully accept, that the true purpose of life for all human beings is to seek God.

In pursuit of that goal, I offer my own life unreservedly to seeking my own Divine Source.

I will retain no ego-gratifying goal in my life, but will strive always, and above all, to please God.

I will view my partner as a channel of God's blessing, guidance, and strength, and will strive always to be a similar channel in return.

I will endeavor always, through the love and respect I feel for my partner, to reach out in love and service to all humanity.

I will try never to see anything in this world as mine, but will view everything as a manifestation of God.

I will look upon life as God's dream-drama, and also dream-entertainment. I will accept as His gift whatever comes to me in life.

I offer to Thee, Lord, my life, my desires, my attachments, and the fruit of all my labors.

Bless me, and strengthen me, that I become ever more perfect in this, my holy vow.

The Pilgrim's Vow of Intention

I understand, and intend from now on to live by my understanding, that life is a pilgrimage, of which the final goal is to find and merge back into God.

I will endeavor resolutely, therefore, to direct all my thoughts and actions toward that end.

I will offer up all material desires for purification in the fire of divine bliss.

I will offer up all attachments for purification in that cosmic fire.

I will search my heart daily for any lingering desires and attachments, and will offer them to Thee, my Cosmic Beloved.

I will strive to be an example to others of a pure, discriminating, and noble life.

I will offer the fruit of all my actions and labors to Thee alone.

Bless me, and direct my footsteps ever to the summit of Thy holy mountain.

Vow of Complete Renunciation

From now on, I embrace as the only purpose of my life the search for God.

I will never take a partner, or, if I am married, I will look upon my partner as belonging only to Thee, Lord. In any case, I am complete in myself, and in myself will merge all the opposites of duality.

I no longer exist as a separate entity, but offer my life unreservedly into Thy great Ocean of Awareness.

I accept nothing as mine, no one as mine, no talent, no success, no achievement as my own, but everything as Thine alone.

I will feel that not only the fruit of my labor, but the labor itself, is only Thine. Act through me always, Lord, to accomplish Thy design.

I am free in Thy joy, and will rejoice forever in Thy blissful presence.

Help me in my efforts to achieve perfection in this, my holy vow. For I have no goal in life but to know Thee, and to serve as Thy channel of blessing to all mankind.

Chapter Eighteen

An Invitation to Swamis

I would like here to extend an invitation to all swamis who feel in tune with the ideals expressed in this book, to join hands with us, wherever they live, in launching this new movement of renunciation.

I think the reason the monastic life has become so generally shunned these days is that renunciation, as it was presented in the past, no longer appeals to people in this new age of greater freedom of thought, conscience, and consciousness. My deep hope is that, as I've presented this new renunciate order, many more people will feel inspired to give their lives to God.

One thought has worried me about this order: If our New-Age Renunciate Order should radiate outward only from the communities of Ananda, might there develop, in time, a tendency to institutionalize the whole order? Were that to happen, it might undermine everything I have tried to begin. This movement is not *my* movement. It is not *Ananda's* movement. I have proposed that Paramhansa Yogananda be accepted by nayaswamis as the adi-guru of this order. I would in fact like for that to happen. But I don't want to approach the Order to the slightest degree as something sectarian. It should become sufficiently widespread to effect a broad change in society. For I deeply feel that this movement can help to uplift the world.

I would like, therefore, as I said, to extend an invitation to all swamis today, provided they endorse the principles I have outlined in this book. I invite you to join us, and to become nayaswamis also. You can be a member of any other organization, provided only that you endorse these ideas.

How would you join this order? I cannot see you ignoring the vows I've proposed. They should be honored by all who call themselves nayaswamis. Adi Shankara had four different maths and ten *dasanamis*. That was because, in his day, even relatively small distances seemed very far. Such separate designations are no longer necessary in this age, when email makes instant communication possible at great distances.

Incidentally, now may be a good time for me to share openly a belief I have long held: namely, that my own Guru, Paramhansa Yogananda, was, in a past incarnation, adi Swami Shankara himself. He often spoke to me personally about that great reforming master, and told me stories that, I think, don't even exist in the known lore about him. One such story, incidentally, was common knowledge among the disciples of my line of gurus; it concerns Shankara's meeting with Babaji (of our line), and acceptance from him of Kriya Yoga initiation.

Other reasons for my belief are more personal. One does not speak easily, however, of these matters. Suffice it to say that I think I was with him then.

To return to the issue at hand: If you yourself are a swami, and if you are in tune with the ideals I've expressed in this book, you may join this new renunciate order no matter where you live. Pilgrims, tyagis, and brahmacharis (and their feminine counterparts, obviously) could be developed, under your guidance, in any organization to which you belong. All I ask is that you write to me (at nayaswami@nayaswami.org).

With a little correspondence, we could arrive at a clear understanding of how this might all be arranged.

I feel right about letting your present status as a swami require no new initiation. All I'd ask of you is, as I said, that you endorse the above principles, sign a pledge (for your own keeping) to abide by this vow of full renunciation, and change your orange habit to a bright royal blue one. After that, it is between you and God. I don't want to have to enter the picture. This is *your* order, and God's order—not mine.

I add again, also, my prayer that we work together to change and uplift the consciousness on our poor, suffering planet.

With unceasing blessings, in divine friendship,
Swami Kriyananda Giri
Nayaswami Kriyananda

Appendix

Married Swamis

by Tyagi Jayadev

In Yogananda's *Autobiography of a Yogi* we read about a historic event at the Kumbha Mela (a religious fair that occurs every several years), when Babaji made Sri Yukteswar a swami. This happened in 1894, during Lahiri Mahasaya's life, according to *The Holy Science*.

Further on in *Autobiography of a Yogi* we read that Sri Yukteswar was later formally and officially initiated in Bodh Gaya: "After my wife died, I joined the Swami Order and received the new name of Yukteswar Giri." That event, as we read, happened *after* Lahiri Mahasaya's death—after September, 1895—as Yogananda indicates in a footnote, explaining that "Yukteswar" was his guru's monastic name, and was "not received by my guru during Lahiri Mahasaya's lifetime."

Studying these quotes, we realize with surprise that when Babaji made Sri Yukteswar a swami at the Kumbha Mela, his wife was still alive: he was still a married man! Babaji, then, made Sri Yukteswar a "married swami"! Sri Yukteswar, back then, called himself more fittingly, "Priya Nath Swami." This was a name he also used when presenting himself in his book, *The Holy Science*. Priya Nath was his family name.

Swami Prajnananda wrote: "Swami Shriyukteswarji was initiated into sannyas by Swami Krishna Dayal Giri of Bodhgaya, on Guru Purnima (full moon day) of July in 1906." Sri Yukteswar presented himself as a married swami for twelve years.

117

Interestingly too, Yogananda made Rajarshi Janakananda a swami, giving him in 1951 the orange robe and a swami name, complete with vow and ceremony, while Rajarshi was a married man. His wife Frieda died after him. She, according to Durga Ma's book, was the reason why Rajarshi ended up being buried not in Los Angeles, next to his guru, but in Kansas. In short, Paramhansa Yogananda made Rajarshi, too, a "married swami."

Our line of gurus, then—Babaji, Lahiri Mahasaya, Sri Yukteswar, and Paramhansa Yogananda—didn't follow the more orthodox definitions of what it means to be a swami.

About the Author

"Swami Kriyananda is a man of wisdom and compassion in action, truly one of the leading lights in the spiritual world today."
—Lama Surya Das, Dzogchen Center, author of *Awakening The Buddha Within*

Swami Kriyananda

A prolific author, accomplished composer, playwright, and artist, and a world-renowned spiritual teacher, Swami Kriyananda refers to himself simply as "a humble disciple" of the great God-realized master, Paramhansa Yogananda. He met his guru at the age of twenty-two, and served him during the last four years of the Master's life. And he has done so continuously ever since.

Kriyananda was born in Rumania of American parents, and educated in Europe, England, and the

United States. Philosophically and artistically inclined from youth, he soon came to question life's meaning, and society's values. During a period of intense inward reflection, he discovered Yogananda's *Autobiography of a Yogi*, and immediately traveled three thousand miles from New York to California to meet the Master, who accepted him as a monastic disciple. Yogananda appointed him as the head of the monastery, authorized him to teach in his name and to give initiation into Kriya Yoga, and entrusted him with the missions of writing, lecturing, and developing what he called "world brotherhood colonies."

Recognized as "the father of the spiritual communities movement" in the United States, Swami Kriyananda founded Ananda World Brotherhood Village in the Sierra Nevada Foothills of Northern California in 1968. It has served as a model for seven communities founded subsequently in the United States, Europe, and India.

In 2003 Swami Kriyananda, then in his seventy-eighth year, moved to India with a small international group of disciples to dedicate his remaining years to making his guru's teachings better known in that country. He has established Ananda's third publishing company, all of which publish his one hundred-plus literary works and spread the teachings of Kriya Yoga throughout the world. His vision for the upcoming years includes, in India, founding cooperative spiritual communities (two communities already exist there, one in Gurgaon and the other near Pune); a temple of all religions dedicated to Yogananda; a retreat center; a school system; a monastery; as well as a university-level Yoga Institute of Living Wisdom.

Further Explorations

If you would like to learn more about Paramhansa Yogananda and his teachings, or about Swami Kriyananda, Crystal Clarity Publishers offers many additional resources to assist you.

Crystal Clarity publishes the original 1946, unedited edition of Paramhansa Yogananda's spiritual masterpiece

Autobiography of a Yogi
Paramhansa Yogananda

Autobiography of a Yogi is one of the bestselling Eastern philosophy titles of all time, with millions of copies sold, named one of the best and most influential books of the twentieth century. This highly prized reprinting of the original 1946 edition is the only one available free from textual changes made after Yogananda's death. Yogananda was the first yoga master of India whose mission was to live and teach in the West.

In this updated edition are bonus materials, including a last chapter that Yogananda wrote in 1951, without posthumous changes. This new edition also includes the eulogy that Yogananda wrote for Gandhi, and a new foreword and afterword by Swami Kriyananda, one of Yogananda's close, direct disciples.

PRAISE FOR *Autobiography of a Yogi*
"In the original edition, published during Yogananda's life, one is more in contact with Yogananda himself. While Yogananda founded centers and organizations, his concern was more with guiding individuals to direct communion with Divinity rather than with promoting any one church as opposed to another. This spirit is easier to grasp in the original edition of this great spiritual and yogic classic."
—David Frawley, Director, American Institute of Vedic
   Studies, author, *Yoga and Ayurveda*

Also available in the following formats:
Unabridged Audiobook *MP3 format*
Card Deck *52 cards and booklet*

A Marvelous Sequel to Autobiography of a Yogi

The New Path
My Life with Paramhansa Yogananda
Swami Kriyananda

The New Path tells the story of a young American's spiritual quest, his discovery of the powerful classic, *Autobiography of a Yogi*, and his subsequent meeting with—and acceptance as a disciple by—the book's author, the great spiritual teacher and yoga master, Paramhansa Yogananda.

The New Path provides a marvelous sequel to Paramhansa Yogananda's own *Autobiography of a Yogi*, helping you to gain a more profound understanding of this great world teacher. Through hundreds of stories of life with Yogananda and through Swami Kriyananda's invaluable insights, you'll discover the inner path that leads to soul-freedom and lasting happiness.

Praise for *The New Path*

"Reading Autobiography of a Yogi *by Yogananda was a transformative experience for me and for millions of others. In* The New Path, *Kriyananda carries on this great tradition. Highly recommended."*

—Dean Ornish, M.D., Founder and President, Preventative Medicine Research Institute, Clinical Professor of Medicine, University of California, San Francisco, author, *The Spectrum*

"Not only did Kriyananda walk in the footsteps of an enlightened master, The New Path *makes it obvious that he himself became an embodiment of Yogananda's teachings."*

—Michael Bernard Beckwith, featured contributor to The Secret, author, *Spiritual Liberation—Fulfilling Your Soul's Potential*

Also available in the following formats:
Unabridged Audiobook *MP3 format*

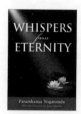

Whispers from Eternity
Paramhansa Yogananda
Edited by His Disciple, Swami Kriyananda

Many poetic works can inspire, but few, like this one, have the power to change your life. Yogananda was not only a spiritual master, but a master poet, whose poems revealed the hidden divine presence behind even everyday things.

Open this book, pick a poem at random, and read it. Mentally repeat whatever phrase appeals to you. Within a short time, you will feel your consciousness transformed. This book has the power to rapidly accelerate your spiritual growth, and provides hundreds of delightful ways for you to begin your own conversation with God.

Also available in the following formats:
Unabridged Audiobook *MP3 format*

The Essence of the Bhagavad Gita
Explained by Paramhansa Yogananda
As Remembered by His Disciple, Swami Kriyananda

Rarely in a lifetime does a new spiritual classic appear that has the power to change people's lives and transform future generations. This is such a book.

This revelation of India's best-loved scripture approaches it from a fresh perspective, showing its deep allegorical meaning and its down-to-earth practicality. The themes presented are universal: how to achieve victory in life in union with the divine; how to prepare for life's "final exam," death, and what happens afterward; how to triumph over all pain and suffering.

PRAISE FOR *The Essence of the Bhagavad Gita*

"The Essence of the Bhagavad Gita *is a brilliant text that will greatly enhance the spiritual life of every reader."*

—Caroline Myss, author of *Anatomy of the Spirit* and *Sacred Contracts*

"It is doubtful that there has been a more important spiritual writing in the last fifty years than this soul-stirring, monumental work. What a gift! What a treasure!"

—Neale Donald Walsch, author of *Conversations with God*

The Wisdom of Yogananda Series

This series features writings of Paramhansa Yogananda not available elsewhere. These books include writings from his earliest years in America, in an approachable, easy-to-read format. The words of the Master are presented with minimal editing to capture Yogananda's wisdom, his sense of fun, and his practical spiritual guidance.

How to Be Happy All the Time
The Wisdom of Yogananda Series, Volume 1
Paramhansa Yogananda

Yogananda powerfully explains virtually everything needed to lead a happier, more fulfilling life. Topics include: looking for happiness in the right places; choosing to be happy; tools and techniques for achieving happiness; sharing happiness with others; balancing success and happiness, and many more.

Karma and Reincarnation
The Wisdom of Yogananda Series, Volume 2
Paramhansa Yogananda

Yogananda reveals the truth behind karma, death, reincarnation, and the afterlife. With clarity and simplicity, he makes the mysterious understandable. Topics include: why we see a world of suffering and inequality; how to handle the challenges in our lives; what happens at death, and after death; and the origin and purpose of reincarnation.

Spiritual Relationships
The Wisdom of Yogananda Series, Volume 3
Paramhansa Yogananda

Topics include: how to cure bad habits that spell the death of true friendship; how to choose the right partner and create a lasting marriage; sex in marriage and how to conceive a spiritual child; problems that arise in marriage and what to do about them; the divine plan uniting parents and children; the Universal Love behind all your relationships.

How to Be a Success
The Wisdom of Yogananda Series, Volume 4
Paramhansa Yogananda

This book includes the complete text of *The Attributes of Success*, the original booklet later published as *The Law of Success*. In addition, you will learn how to find your purpose in life, develop habits of success and eradicate habits of failure, develop your will power and magnetism, and thrive in the right job.

How to Have Courage, Calmness, & Confidence
The Wisdom of Yogananda Series, Volume 5
Paramhansa Yogananda

Courage, calmness, and confidence are the secrets to dealing with any challenge life sends. The "impossible" becomes manageable, and a steppingstone to greater inner strength. Everyone can be courageous, calm, and confident, because these are qualities of the soul. Hypnotized with material thinking and desires, we've lost touch with our indomitable soul force.

In this potent book of the highest spiritual wisdom, Yogananda shares the most practical steps for reconnecting with your own soul. Topics include: access courage, calmness, and confidence; overcome the great obstacles: worry, fear, nervousness, and anger; use scientific healing affirmations to transform your thinking and energy; concentrate and meditate to attune to the natural soul force within you.

The Essence of Self-Realization
The Wisdom of Paramhansa Yogananda
Recorded, Compiled, & Edited by His Disciple,
Swami Kriyananda

With nearly three hundred sayings rich with spiritual wisdom, this book is the fruit of a labor of love. A glance at the table of contents will convince the reader of the vast scope of this book. It offers as complete an explanation of life's true purpose, and of the way to achieve that purpose, as may be found anywhere.

Religion in the New Age
Swami Kriyananda

Our planet has entered an "Age of Energy" that will affect us for centuries to come. We can see evidence of this all around us: in ultra-fast computers, the quickening of communication and transportation, and the shrinking of time and space. This fascinating book of essays explores how this new age will change our lives, especially our spiritual seeking. Covers a wide range of upcoming societal shifts—in leadership, relationships, and self-development—including the movement away from organized religion to inner experience.

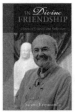

In Divine Friendship
Swami Kriyananda

This extraordinary book of nearly 250 letters, written over a thirty-year period by Swami Kriyananda, responds to practically any concern a spiritual seeker might have, such as: strengthening one's faith, accelerating one's spiritual progress, meditating more deeply, responding to illness, earning a living, attracting a mate, raising children, overcoming negative self-judgments, and responding to world upheavals.

Connecting all of these letters is the love, compassion, and wisdom of Swami Kriyananda, one of the leading spiritual figures of our times. The letters describe in detail his efforts to fulfill his Guru's commission to establish spiritual communities, and offer invaluable advice to leaders everywhere on how to avoid the temptations of materialism, selfishness, and pride. A spiritual treasure that speaks to truth seekers at all levels.

Meditation for Starters
Swami Kriyananda

Have you wanted to learn to meditate, but just never got around to it? Or tried "sitting in the silence" only to find yourself too restless to stay more than a few moments? If so, *Meditation for Starters* is just what you've been looking for; and with a companion CD, it provides everything you need to begin a meditation practice. It is filled with easy-to-follow instructions, beautiful guided visualizations, and answers to important questions on meditation, such as: what meditation is (and isn't); how to relax your body and prepare yourself for going within; and techniques for interiorizing and focusing the mind.

Awaken to Superconsciousness
How to Use Meditation for Inner Peace,
Intuitive Guidance, and Greater Awareness
Swami Kriyananda

This popular guide includes everything you need to know about the philosophy and practice of meditation, and how to apply the meditative mind to resolving common daily conflicts in uncommon, superconscious ways. Superconsciousness is the source of intuition, spiritual healing, solutions to problems, and deep and lasting joy.

Praise for *Awaken to Superconsciousness*

"*A brilliant, thoroughly enjoyable guide to the art and science of meditation. [Kriyananda] entertains, informs, and inspires—his enthusiasm for the subject is contagious. This book is a joy to read from beginning to end.*"
— *Yoga International*

Also available in the following formats:
Music to Awaken Superconsciousness *CD*
Meditations to Awaken Superconsiousness, *spoken word CD*

127

Music and Audiobook Selections

 ## Metaphysical Meditations
Swami Kriyananda

Kriyananda's soothing voice guides you in thirteen different meditations based on the soul-inspiring, mystical poetry of Paramhansa Yogananda. Each meditation is accompanied by beautiful classical music to help you quiet your thoughts and prepare for deep states of meditation. Includes a full recitation of Yogananda's poem "Samadhi," which appears in *Autobiography of a Yogi*. A great aid to the serious meditator, as well as to those just beginning their practice.

 ## Meditations to Awaken Superconsciousness
Guided Meditations on the Light
Swami Kriyananda

Featuring two beautiful guided meditations as well as an introductory section to help prepare the listener for meditation, this extraordinary recording of visualizations can be used either by itself, or as a companion to the book, *Awaken to Superconsciousness*. The soothing, transformative words, spoken over inspiring sitar background music, creates one of the most unique guided meditation products available.

Bliss Chants
Ananda Kirtan

Chanting focuses and lifts the mind to higher states of consciousness. *Bliss Chants* features chants written by Yogananda and his direct disciple, Swami Kriyananda. They're performed by Ananda Kirtan, a group of singers and musicians from Ananda, one of the world's most respected yoga communities. Chanting is accompanied by guitar, harmonium, kirtals, and tabla.

Other titles in the Chant Series:

Divine Mother Chants	Power Chants
Love Chants	Peace Chants
Wisdom Chants*	Wellness Chants*

AUM: Mantra of Eternity
Swami Kriyananda

This recording features nearly seventy minutes of continuous vocal chanting of AUM, the Sanskrit word meaning peace and oneness of spirit. AUM, the cosmic creative vibration, is extensively discussed by Yogananda in *Autobiography of a Yogi*. Chanted here by his disciple, Kriyananda, this recording is a stirring way to tune into this cosmic power.

Other titles in the Mantra Series:
Gayatri Mantra*
Mahamrityanjaya Mantra*
Maha Mantra*

Relax: Meditations for Flute and Cello
Donald Walters
Featuring David Eby and Sharon Nani

This CD is specifically designed to slow respiration and heart rate, bringing listeners to their calm center. This recording features fifteen melodies for flute and cello, accompanied by harp, guitar, keyboard, and strings. Excellent for creating a calming atmosphere for work and home.

Visit our website to view all our available titles in books, audiobooks, spoken word, music and DVDs.

www.crystalclarity.com

*Titles will be available starting summer 2010

Crystal Clarity Publishers

When you're seeking a book on practical spiritual living, you want to know it's based on an authentic tradition of timeless teachings, and that it resonates with integrity. This is the goal of Crystal Clarity Publishers: to offer you books of practical wisdom filled with true spiritual principles that have not only been tested through the ages, but also through personal experience.

We publish only books that combine creative thinking, universal principles, and a timeless message. Crystal Clarity books will open doors to help you discover more fulfillment and joy by living and acting from the center of peace within you.

Crystal Clarity Publishers—recognized worldwide for its bestselling, original, unaltered edition of Paramhansa Yogananda's classic *Autobiography of a Yogi*—offers many additional resources to assist you in your spiritual journey, including over ninety books, a wide variety of inspirational and relaxation music composed by Swami Kriyananda, Yogananda's direct disciple, and yoga and meditation DVDs.

For our online catalog, complete with secure ordering, please visit us on the web at:

www.crystalclarity.com

We offer many of our book titles in unabridged MP3 format audiobooks. To purchase these titles and to see more music and audiobook offerings, visit our website www.crystalclarity.com. Or look for us in many of the popular online download sites.

To request a catalog, place an order for the products you read about in the Further Explorations section of this book, or to find out more information about us and our products, please contact us:

Contact Information
14618 Tyler Foote Rd. • Nevada City, CA 95959
t: 800-424-1055 or 530-478-7600
w: www.crystalclarity.com
e: clarity@crystalclarity.com

Ananda Sangha

Ananda Sangha is a fellowship of kindred souls following the teachings of Paramhansa Yogananda. The Sangha embraces the search for higher consciousness through the practice of meditation, and through the ideal of service to others in their quest for Self-realization. Approximately ten thousand spiritual seekers are affiliated with Ananda Sangha throughout the world.

Founded in 1968 by Swami Kriyananda, a direct disciple of Paramhansa Yogananda, Ananda includes seven communities in the United States, Europe, and in India. Worldwide, about one thousand devotees live in these spiritual communities, which are based on Yogananda's ideals of "plain living and high thinking."

"Thousands of youths must go north, south, east and west to cover the earth with little colonies, demonstrating that simplicity of living plus high thinking lead to the greatest happiness!" After pronouncing these words at a garden party in Beverly Hills, California in 1949, Paramhansa Yogananda raised his arms, and chanting the sacred cosmic vibration AUM, he "registered in the ether" his blessings on what has become the spiritual communities movement. From that moment on, Swami Kriyananda dedicated himself to bringing this vision from inspiration to reality by establishing communities where home, job, school, worship, family, friends, and recreation could evolve together as part of the interwoven fabric of harmonious, balanced living. Yogananda predicted that these communities would "spread like wildfire," becoming the model lifestyle for the coming millennium.

Swami Kriyananda lived with his guru during the last four years of the Master's life, and continued to serve his organization for another ten years, bringing the teachings of Kriya Yoga and Self-realization to audiences in the United States, Europe, Australia, and, from 1958–1962, India. In 1968, together with a small group of close friends and students, he founded the first "world-brotherhood community" in the foothills of the Sierra Nevada Mountains in northeastern California. Initially a meditation retreat located on sixty-seven acres of forested land, Ananda World Brotherhood Village today encompasses one thousand acres where about 250 people live a dynamic, fulfilling life based on the principles and practices of spiritual, mental, and physical development, cooperation, respect, and divine friendship.

At this writing, after forty years of existence, Ananda is one of the most successful networks of intentional communities in the world. Urban communities have been developed in Palo Alto and Sacramento, California; Portland, Oregon; and Seattle, Washington. In Europe, near Assisi, Italy, a spiritual retreat and community was established in 1983, where today nearly one hundred residents from eight countries live. In Pune and Gurgaon, India there are two communities and a spiritual retreat center.

Contact Information

Ananda Sangha

mail: 14618 Tyler Foote Rd. • Nevada City, CA 95959
phone: 530-478-7560
online: www.ananda.org
email: sanghainfo@ananda.org

The E xpanding Light

Ananda's non-profit guest retreat, The Expanding Light, is visited by over two thousand people each year. We offer a varied, year-round schedule of classes and workshops on yoga, meditation, spiritual practices, yoga and meditation teacher training, and personal renewal retreats. The Expanding Light welcomes seekers from all backgrounds. Here you will find a loving, accepting environment, ideal for personal growth and spiritual renewal.

We strive to create an ideal relaxing and supportive environment for people to explore their own spiritual growth. We share the nonsectarian meditation practices and yoga philosophy of Paramhansa Yogananda and his direct disciple, Ananda's founder, Swami Kriyananda. Yogananda called his path "Self-realization," and our goal is to help our guests tune into their own higher Selves.

Contact Information

Expanding Light

*mail:*14618 Tyler Foote Rd. • Nevada City, CA 95959
phone: 800-346-5350
online: www.expandinglight.org
email: info@expandinglight.org